4/2013
#13⁰⁰
A
650
MAS

DATE DUE

MAY 0 4 2013			
GAYLORD			PRINTED IN U.S.A.

Six Lessons for Six Sons

SIX LESSONS

FOR SIX SONS

AN EXTRAORDINARY FATHER, A SIMPLE FORMULA FOR SUCCESS

JOE MASSENGALE

AND DAVID CLOW

THREE RIVERS PRESS
NEW YORK

Published in the United States by Three Rivers Press, an imprint of the
Crown Publishing Group, a division of Random House, Inc., New York.
www.crownpublishing.com

Three Rivers Press and the Tugboat design are registered trademarks of
Random House, Inc.

Originally published in hardcover in the United States by Harmony Books,
an imprint of the Crown Publishing Group, a division of Random House, Inc.,
New York, in 2006.

Library of Congress Cataloging-in-Publication Data
Massengale, Joe.
    Six lessons for six sons: an extraordinary father, a simple formula
for success / Joe Massengale and David Clow.
        1. Massengale, Joe.   2. African Americans—Biography.   3. African
American fathers—Biography.   4. African American businesspeople—
California—Biography.   5. Successful people—United States—
Biography.   6. Fathers and sons—United States.   7. African American
men—Conduct of life.   8. Character.   9. Success—United States.
10. Values—United States.   I. Clow, David.   II. Title.
    E185.97.M375A3   2005
    650.1089'96073—dc22   2005027773

ISBN   978-0-307-23811-5

Printed in the United States of America

DESIGN BY BARBARA STURMAN

10 9 8 7 6 5 4 3 2 1

First Paperback Edition

Contents

FOREWORD

by George Foreman

I'VE HAD three careers: boxer, preacher, and businessman. Four, if you count my misspent youth. In all four, I learned something valuable.

In each career I had setbacks and triumph. I've been blessed to know the greatest victories a man can ask for, and I've felt the sting of humbling defeat. As a boxer, I won and lost and won and lost again as heavyweight champion; as a preacher, I knew the rewards and sacrifices of sharing the Word; and as an entrepreneur, I face the same challenges any businessman faces to keep customers happy.

My life is an uncommon one, but the successes I've enjoyed all had some simple common elements that can be shared no matter what you do or where you start. In every case, it was character that helped me win. Character is the tenacity to fail, learn and come back stronger. It is the grace to win with humility, to lose with dignity and to give your best in both. It is being honest with yourself, to listen only for the very best within you, seeking to improve who you are and what you do, to leave things better than you found them.

It surprises me sometimes that such a practical thing as character isn't taught alongside accounting and finance and marketing in business schools, because I've never seen a business succeed without it. Many business disappointments happen because the personal qualities of character somehow got lost inside a company, and seemingly successful people reveal themselves to be spiritually bankrupt. As these people learned the techniques for accumulating earthly treasures, they lost the real meaning of living well and doing good work. If you define success too narrowly, you can succeed beyond your wildest dreams while losing your family, betraying your customers and leaving nothing behind but personal tragedy.

I try to keep this in my heart always in my most important work, being a father. My ten children have their own lives, their own paths to follow as they choose their careers and move out into the world. The specifics of my life might be of value to them, but none of my kids is likely to duplicate my path. My fights will not be theirs. The most valuable things I can give them are the simplest ones: a father's love; trust in God's grace and His hopes for them; and the character that will equip them to build good lives, good businesses and good families.

In this I have much in common with Joe Massengale. We come from the same part of East Texas. Our families worked the same land in Marshall, where I live today. We both know what it feels like to be hungry, to wear old clothes and cardboard in our shoes. We know the feeling of having to move house to house, and of being judged for having too little. We also know what it's like to want more, and not to wait for opportunity but to make our own. We know the ambition to achieve something for our families, the drive to be successes in our businesses and the importance of doing things right.

Confidence, fortitude, pride, persistence, fearlessness and focus are some of the true treasures of the spirit that can get you past defeat, help you build a business, raise a family and leave a valuable legacy. The lessons Joe Massengale learned back in the piney woods around Marshall and gave to his sons to take into the world are some of the same ones I hope my children, my congregation, the kids in my youth center and my customers get from me.

Bestselling author, ordained minister, and two-time heavyweight boxing champion, George Foreman is the founder of the George Foreman Youth and Community Center. The father of ten children, he lives with his family in Texas.

Six Lessons for Six Sons

INTRODUCTION

ON JULY 7, 2000, Marshall, Texas, witnessed a homecoming and a rite of passage, a reconciliation and a recognition of how the world changes. Joe Massengale, Sr., was back for his induction into the local Hall of Fame.

Marshall is a midsize Texas town three hours east of Dallas, but some of its children are known around the globe. Lady Bird Johnson is from Marshall. So are journalist Bill Moyers, who revisited in the mid-1980s to make a documentary, *Marshall, Texas; Marshall, Texas,* about the still-divided soul of the city more than a century after the Civil War; former heavyweight champion boxer George Foreman, who runs his thriving food and consumer products company from a 300-acre ranch northeast of the town; football quarterback Y. A. Tittle; and civil rights leader James Leonard Farmer. Like Joe Massengale, they left home to make their fortunes, and each in his or her own way acknowledged the lessons Marshall taught them by donating personal effects to the Hall.

The observance in the historic Harrison County Courthouse saluted a man with none of the natural gifts of the athletes or the education of the scholars. Joe had only his character to help him in life. That day, a heavyweight champion and a president's wife and a broadcast journalist were joined in Marshall's heart by a tree trimmer, who, when he got back to Los Angeles from the celebration, would be out in his truck again selling his services door-to-door. But ultimately, Joe Massengale's effect on the world may be the greatest of all. He left Texas with nothing and came home to Texas a winner. His gifts to Marshall were the tangible signs of just how powerful the American dream can be if one lives it every day.

Some of the greatest success stories America has are the quietest ones. Joe Massengale's story of achievement took him from fear to hope and from hunger to abundance. It is more powerful because it is shared by so many people like Joe.

Best of all, Joe's story is only a beginning. He has six exemplary sons, Joe Jr., Michael, Larry, Randy, Patrick and Andre. They gathered from around the country to be with him that day in East Texas. Even his sons did not fully understand until then how far their father had come, or all that his journey meant.

Marshall's pride for its son and grandsons was genuine, and Joe himself was so moved he could barely speak. Hanging in the same gallery as Y. A. Tittle's number 14 New York Giants jersey and the mementos from Moyers and Foreman and the First Lady are memorabilia from Joe Massengale's careers. He donated flyers from Joe's Expert Tree Service, the first African-American–owned landscaping company to succeed in Beverly Hills. He offered clippings from his work as a disk jockey and record producer in Los Angeles. From his racing days, Joe gave silks in the lavender and gold colors of Pemberton High, the school in Marshall where he announced one day to the classmates who laughed at his poverty that he was going to Los Angeles to get rich and someday he'd come back in triumph.

The mayor proclaimed it Joe Massengale Day, and friends from Joe's childhood joined city officials to pay their respects. *The Marshall News-Messenger* called him "a Horatio Alger story." Joe was photographed with the statue of Lady Justice, brought down for restoration from her place atop the cupola of the Courthouse.

After the ceremonies, Joe showed his sons the spot in Courthouse Square where he used to shine shoes for nickels, and the road in the piney woods outside the town where, at age eight, he saw a man shot and dragged to death, and the thirty acres he took over at twelve when his father, Hugh Massengale, had to leave the family six days a week to find work where he could get it. Joe took his sons to the little graveyard where he buried Hugh in 1945. He had warned them about snakes in the undergrowth—this is rattler country—but the Massengale brothers wanted to see where Hugh lay to better understand the things Joe's father had taught him, and how Joe was able to pass those things on.

"I SHOULDN'T even be here," Joe Massengale says. "It's a blessing that I'm alive to tell you this. So many people like me didn't make it."

At seventy-seven Joe looks sixty, with smooth skin, salt-and-pepper hair and a trimmed mustache. He smiles as he shows the clippings and photos from the celebration in Marshall. He tells this story from the sunny kitchen of his house in the Baldwin Hills section of Los Angeles.

Joe lives alone, but his house is immaculate inside and out. His photos from the winner's circle at Santa Anita and Hollywood Park, and from his career in music, line the study. The windows look out onto a putting-green lawn, trimmed ficus trees and his prized midnight-blue Cadillac at the curb. His brown Rolls-Royce sits in the garage. Joe shows the Rolls with particular pride. When he went to buy it, he was wearing workman's coveralls after trimming trees all day. The salesman at the dealership asked him if he was there to see the janitor. Joe paid for the car in cash.

"My father was Hugh T. Massengale," Joe says. "He was born in 1880 in Jefferson, Texas, north of Marshall. Jim Crow years. Slavery, almost. Worse than slavery, in some ways. At least if you were property, somebody had an interest in protecting you. It wasn't that way afterwards. People got killed for nothing all the time.

"My dad roamed around Texas, making a living by laboring or barbering. Married his first wife, the one before my mother, when he was a young man. I don't know much about my dad's first marriage. I never met his first sons. His eldest son was a boy named Horace T. Massengale. Horace worked in the jewelry store in Marshall. He went swimming with White boys there. Horace thought he could trust them, I guess, but it was said they drowned him for being too friendly with the White girls. That hurt my father quite a bit. He used to warn us all the time about that. You couldn't do that. Hugh himself was almost killed by a lynch mob when I was just a kid.

"It was hell what a person endured then, and even in my time. Unbelievable. You can't imagine what Black people went through. The books talk about it but living it . . . *man.* My life might have ended right there in Marshall. So I mean it, I'm blessed to be here.

"My dad went to Marshall and got into contracting and logging. They made him head of a crew. That's when he met my mother, Susie Walton. Tall Indian-looking girl, very pretty. He married her when she was seventeen. He was thirty-five or so. Her father went looking for my dad with a shotgun and my dad had to show him the marriage papers to keep Susie's father from killing him.

"He hung in there in East Texas after that because he had a wife. They started a family, and my dad worked all the time. All the time. Winter, summer, hurt or not, just work. Logging and filing saws and farming. He and a man were chopping a big log once and my dad took the ax right in the knee. Almost took his leg right off. The man ran. My father had to yell after him, 'Stay here with me, stay here and help me!' They put him on a log truck and took him to the doctor. Doctor sewed it up best he could. My dad had a limp after that, but he couldn't stop working. Not with kids to feed. Bob. Alzie. Fred. Herbert. Oliver. Olivia. Ollie. Then me. Then the little ones, Alfred, Lendell, Idell and Willie Ruth, and the baby we called Little Brother.

"We lived all over the area in and around Marshall. The house I was born in is gone now. We tried finding it when we were back there for the Hall of Fame ceremony. You can't tell a house was ever there. The spot is grown over with trees a hundred feet tall.

"Here's the way people built a house like that. You'd get the straightest slabs of lumber you could get at the logging mill. You'd nail those planks up to a wood frame. Then you'd go to the fields and pull up the long grass, waist high or so, tall blades. You'd get you a lot of that tall grass. And you'd get some white mud and some sand, and you'd put it all in a tub with water and make a thick paste, and then paste the cracks in the lumber. That was your house. Now, that grass got dry as tinder in the walls, and when I was just three or four days old, my mother was cooking and the house caught fire. Dad saw it from the field and came running. There were people coming by on wagons and they tried to help put it out, but the water was a ways from the house. Wasn't any chance of saving it, it burned so fast. I was sleeping on a hay mattress, and my dad grabbed it and folded it double with me in it—he didn't even know I was there, he was just trying to save anything he could save—and he tossed it out in the ditch. My mother was screaming, *'Where's my baby?'* with the house going up in flames. And I was sleeping on the mattress outside.

"I guess you wonder why I'm like I am today," Joe says with a smile. "So many things could have ended it for me, for my family. I'm blessed. Miracle things happen in life. Miracles."

Miracle things happen in life.

Joe Massengale's life is a series of miracles, from surviving a childhood of poverty to succeeding as a door-to-door tree trimmer to raising six sons during dangerous years in Los Angeles. The Massengales' careers today include real estate and entertainment and technology and home service and catering. Their children are all over the world, building new miracles on the foundation they inherited. Their school for business and for life was Joe's Expert Tree Service.

The details of Joe's life comprise an inspiring tale of success in America, but the real focus of his story is not the past. It's the future. The elements of drive, character and faith that Joe taught his six sons can inspire parents to cultivate themselves as role models. They can help every son and daughter in the next generation of our children to dream great dreams and achieve great things.

Joe Massengale made his miracles into six lessons he could pass along to his family and to you. This book is about those lessons. It shows them in practice, threaded through a century of American history in Joe's life and the lives of his sons, and through the lives of some of our most accomplished role models in business, sports, education and the arts. All these seemingly different people, in so many walks of life, share these timeless lessons of character and wisdom.

This is a quintessentially American story. It begins with a tree trimmer. You can take it anywhere you want to go.

Miracle things happened in Joe Massengale's life because he made them happen. So did the eight accomplished people whose stories parallel Joe's. In *Six Lessons for Six Sons*, they tell you how you can make your life a miracle too.

LESSON ONE

CONFIDENCE

Preface by Guion S. "Guy" Bluford, Jr., Ph.D.

I was fourteen years old in 1957, and a student at Overbrook High School in Philadelphia, when the Soviet Union launched the first satellite, a little silver sphere called Sputnik. It was a startling moment for America, and like the rest of the nation, my family listened with concern to the signal on the radio, a raspy beep beep beep, *as it passed overhead.*

The airplane was invented by Americans. The first pilot to fly the Atlantic solo was American. So was the first to fly over the South Pole. We expected to be the first nation into space. We were wrong.

We were wrong again when I was a freshman at Penn State in April 1961, when Vostok 1 *carried Senior Lieutenant Yuri Gagarin into the first manned Earth orbit. America was humbled. It wasn't just a matter of bragging rights between rival countries. This was the middle of the Cold War. Our leaders viewed supremacy in space as vital to survival on the ground. We had to win because we had to survive. And we were behind.*

Moments like that shook the confidence of the nation. But we came back, daring ourselves to reach and work, to lose for the moment if losses happened, but never to give up. We made fatal mistakes. We lost admirable people on the way. But the impossible goal President Kennedy set for

America, to be on the moon by 1970, became possible by the combination of technical achievement and sheer will.

We might sometimes take for granted today what was so challenging and dangerous at the time. We might assume that because the early explorers made it look easy, it was. If we make the mistake of taking a difficult thing lightly, we miss the point: it's fun to do the hard things. It's fulfilling to set an impossible task and reach it. No one grows by settling for the possible. Nothing gets better by staying the same.

My parents never needed to repeat ideas like this to my brothers and me when we were growing up. They both had master's degrees, and it was understood that we'd all go to college and all seek to stretch ourselves in challenging fields. A counselor once told me that I wasn't college material, perhaps because I wasn't the most enthusiastic reader in high school unless it was something about engineering or math. It might make my story more romantic if I could say I was inspired by being underestimated, and all the more determined to succeed. The truth is, I ignored that counselor. I'd been raised to know what I wanted, and to pursue it no matter what, and I knew I had what I needed. I knew it when I was one of a handful of African-American students at school, and when I was training for combat, and when I wanted to fly on the shuttle. Confidence was my parents' greatest gift. Nothing could take it from me.

This nation could have given up at the sound of that little beep beep beep doing what we'd failed to do in 1957. Instead, we pushed ahead. I might have given up at being told I wouldn't be able to live my dreams. I didn't, and neither should you. Never give up. Never.

I had a moment of free time now and then while looking down from orbit over the earth, riding the space shuttle along the same trajectory as Sputnik *and* Gagarin, *taking the same step that the astronauts before me took to the moon and that the ones to come will take on their way to the stars, to think about the confidence my folks gave me. I knew that that's what put me there. Imagine where it might take you.*

Guy Bluford, Jr., Ph.D., spent fifteen years with NASA as one of its elite astronauts. The first African-American in space, he was inducted into the International Space Hall of Fame in 1997. Today Dr. Bluford serves as president of the Aerospace Technology Group (ATG), an aerospace technology and business consulting organization, and conducts a very active civic life.

JOE MASSENGALE was seven years old when his father left the house one morning to confront Jim Craig over an unpaid debt. Joe's whole life might have changed that day.

"People were murdered for nothing all the time," Joe remembers. "There wasn't any protection for Black folks then. It could happen to any of us in a moment. I remember one man who died by mistake. They thought he'd taken up with a White woman. The killers murdered his brother and left a note: 'Sorry, we got the wrong one.'

"Mister Jim Craig had taken money my dad had earned from growing cotton. Now, Papa was a friendly man, smiling and cheerful. He loved people and mixed easy. But he was a straight man and he had a family to feed, and you couldn't cross him that way. And he was furious. My mother tried to keep him at home—'Hugh, don't you go down there!'—but he left our house and went into Marshall. I followed him."

The confrontation occurred at the most dangerous possible place, the Harrison County Courthouse in the center of town.

"Courthouse Square was where the White men pulled their wagons up and gathered to talk and smoke during the day," Joe says. "Blacks didn't gather here except on Saturday afternoon. There might have been other Black men there that day. But it wouldn't have made any difference.

"There was old Mister Jim, in a straw hat and khaki suit. My father said, 'Mister Jim, I want the money you got from selling my cotton.' Mister Jim said, 'Nigger, get on out of here.' And my daddy knocked him to his knees.

"Around there they lynched Black men who hit a White man. They'd hang them from a tree by the Courthouse and leave the body up overnight. The newspaper would take a picture of it to remind Black folks just what was what around there. And the men ran up and shouted, 'Let's kill this nigger.'"

By 1861, when Texas seceded from the Union, Marshall was one of the largest and most prosperous communities in the state. Known as "the Athens of Texas," it was the cradle of many of the state's most important leaders, a rail center for the nation west of the Mississippi and a key producer of military leadership and supplies for the Confederacy.

Secessionist spirits ran high there. Texas's first and last Confederate governors were from Marshall. The town served as the Confederate capital of the state of Missouri when Missouri itself declined to join the cause. After the fall of Vicksburg in 1863, Marshall was the administrative center of the C.S.A. government in the far west.

The Civil War records of the *Texas Republican*, a local newspaper, tell of Marshall teenagers forming military units and drilling to fight, and of the local women trading recipes for homemade substitutes so they could ship the best food and cloth to the soldiers. Marshall folk learned to tan leather and make cloth shoes so they could get along without imports from the factories in New England. They spun thread and made dyes to weave their own cloth, and turned all their old rags and bedding into first-aid supplies. "Don't forget to save garden seeds," the paper advised, "for if the war continues, it will be impossible to get them next year. Besides, we must, in any event, learn to live without the North." Lincoln was hanged in effigy in Marshall in 1861—"thus," said the newspaper, "would the Abolition President himself be served were he to enter a Southern state."

Confederate Vice President Alexander Stephens, who had served in Congress for Georgia before secession, told listeners in Savannah in 1861 how the new government of the South would be an improvement over the old one. The United States government, he said, had been built "upon the assumption of the equality of races. This was an error. It was a sandy foundation, and the government built upon it fell when the 'storm came and the wind blew.'

"Our new government," Stephens said, "is founded upon exactly the opposite idea; its foundations are laid, its cornerstone rests, upon the great truth that the Negro is not equal to the White man; that slavery—subordination to the superior race—is his natural and normal condition. This, our new government, is the first, in the history of the world, based upon this great physical, philosophical, and moral truth."

Marshall held the largest population of slaves in Texas, Joe Massengale's great-grandparents among them.

▦

THE LAST battle of the Civil War was fought in Texas, at Palmito Ranch east of Brownsville. About three hundred Confederate soldiers led by Colonel John Solomon Ford engaged two Union African-American infantry regiments and a company of cavalry soldiers fighting on foot. The skirmish happened on May 12–13, 1865, more than a month after the formal end of hostilities. The Confederates won. The Union prisoners told them that Robert E. Lee had surrendered to Ulysses S. Grant at Appomattox five weeks earlier.

The war was over. The fight went on.

Before Marshall native Governor Pendleton Murrah fled Texas for Mexico with other C.S.A. officials in 1865, he issued a broadside insisting to his fellow Texans that "you cannot look for relief from emancipation, nor to those other weak and wicked delusions—reconstruction, or a foreign protectorate." Murrah's hometown became a Union base and home to a post of The Bureau of Refugees, Freedmen and Abandoned Lands, better known as the Freedmen's Bureau. Wiley College was founded in Marshall in 1873 to educate the liberated slaves who came to seek a new chance in life. The post–Civil War era brought prosperity to the city, when the voters subsidized a new rail hub for Jay Gould's Texas and Pacific, the eastern end of a proposed line running from Texas to San Diego. Marshall was a busy cotton depot, home to East Texas's first department store, J. Weisman and Co., opened in 1878, the same year Walter Paye Lane, an Irish-born resident and storekeeper who had been an early volunteer on behalf of

Texas in 1861 and who rose to brigadier general in service to the rebellion, led a White supremacist "Citizens Party" in taking control of Marshall, declaring it "redeemed" from its role in the reconstructed Union.

The Harrison County Courthouse, where Joe Massengale watched the angry men surround his father that day, was a beautiful domed structure of golden brick and pink Texas granite, in the center of a broad plaza of hand-laid brick pavement built at the turn of the twentieth century. Decades after the Civil War, the old spirit of the slave days still ran high in Marshall. On the side opposite the spot where Hugh Massengale's life was threatened, the United Daughters of the Confederacy had placed a statue of a young Rebel with musket in 1905, with the inscription "The love, gratitude, and memory of the people of the South shall hold their name in one eternal sunshine" and a poem on the south face of the pedestal:

> Soldier, you in the wreck of gray
> With the brazen belt of the CSA
> Take our love and our tears to-day,
> Take them, all we have to give
> And by God's help while our heart shall live
> It shall keep in its faithful way
> The camp-fires lit for the men in gray
> And the silver bugles of heaven play
> As the roll is called at judgment day.

The Jim Crow years, Hugh Massengale's time, were a deadly era for Texas Blacks. Over 450 victims were lynched in the state during Hugh's lifetime, the overwhelming majority of them African-American. One of the worst concentrations of such killings was Harrison County, and one of the preferred places to make an example of a Black man who got out of line was this very spot on the Courthouse grounds where the men surrounded Hugh as Joe watched. The hanging tree was a pecan, the Texas state tree.

"Mister John Sanders was the sheriff," Joe remembers. "He rode up on horseback. It was sheer luck that he was close enough to make a difference. He saw the crowd, saw Mister Jim Craig laying on the ground. He said, 'What's goin' on around this place?'

"'This nigger hit Mister Jim,' somebody said, 'and we're gonna kill him!'

"Sheriff Sanders saw my dad and said, 'No . . . no, don't you do that. I know this nigger.' He had to say 'nigger'; he couldn't call my father a man. A nigger wasn't a man. Sheriff Sanders said, 'Mister Jim had to have done something to this nigger. He *had* to. Hugh Massengale don't bother nobody.'

"'Nigger,' he told my dad, 'you go on home to your family. Mister Jim, you go on home too.' The White men objected: 'We gon' kill him, nigger hit a White man!' They wanted to get a rope. Sheriff Sanders said, 'No. If it had been any other nigger I'd say go on and lynch him, but Hugh Massengale don't cause no trouble. You all go on home. Go on.' And thank God, that was the end of it."

▦

"WE DID what we had to do," Joe says. "My dad grew corn and cotton, sharecropping thirds and fourths, it was called:

splitting what he grew in thirds and fourths with the owner of the farm. If you supplied all your own mules and wagons and all, you got more. If the owner of the farm supplied the animals and the wagons, you got less, maybe half. My dad always worked on thirds or fourths, not halves. He'd want to keep most of what he grew. Twenty-five dollars for a bale of cotton that might have taken him a year to grow. He earned it.

"We had to move from place to place around the area. One day Dad loaded up all we had in a ten-dollar wagon. We were passing by a vacant house on Hezzie Cook Road on the way to my grandmother's. He knocked on the door and nobody came, and well, we just moved in. Got some water from the well, some soap; we scrubbed the place and patched up the windows and slept on the floor that night. We stayed there three years.

"My dad made seven dollars and fifty cents a week as a contractor, when the work was there. My family could eat a week or even two on that. A sack of meal cost a quarter. Flour was fifty cents for forty pounds. You raised your greens in the backyard. He'd carry a sack of flour and a twenty-five-pound sack of sugar home seven or eight miles. We were glad to have it. He'd buy five bullets a week and get up before dawn every morning and come back with a rabbit or a squirrel. My mother would make some biscuits and gravy for us. Some weeks the work wasn't there, but he'd say, We'll make some money someplace. We all went to work. He hired his sons out to work on farms for different people, filing saws, cutting wood. We got by.

"My dad . . . he had that confidence. That's where I got mine. It was hard all over, yes, but you couldn't just say, 'I'm dead, I might as well turn over.' He showed me how to keep going, no matter what.

"Kids at school would make fun of us. They knew we were hungry. They'd see me barefoot in the springtime, walking miles to get to school, or wearing used women's shoes with the heels knocked off because I didn't have anything else. And they'd laugh about it. To this day I still find myself sitting with my feet tucked under the chair, hiding my shoes because I remember what people said about me. That stayed with me. I told the ones who made fun of me, 'You're all laughing at me now, but my brothers live in California, and one of these days I'm going to Los Angeles and I'm going to get rich. Just watch what I say.' One of them reminded me of it when I went back to Marshall.

"Being made fun of for being poor... that was tough. People shouldn't do that. It's not right. We lived with it all the time, people saying things to us you'd never want to hear; not being able to use the front door at the Paramount Theatre to look at a movie, or eat in a restaurant like anyone else. Some days it seemed like all you could do was give up. But I wouldn't let them make me believe what they said. My dad taught me early: be confident, be careful and make yourself into what you want to be. I believed him. This is America, and you can do that here.

"There's always someone like that, trying to kill your confidence. Doesn't matter where you're from; you see it all the time. We never let it happen to us in my family. My dad told us, 'You have to push yourself. You can't lay back.' I remember being held back in the sixth grade. I wasn't doing my homework like I ought to have been, and I got in to it with the

teacher and she wasn't going to let me go on. Well, the time
came for my classmates in school to start middle school, and I
just went on anyway. I registered just as though I was supposed to, and I started seventh grade. I was embarrassed—I
knew I could do the work. I wasn't going to let someone else
hold me back.

"People like us were country people. The town people
looked down on us. But we all went to high school at Pemberton High in Marshall. Papa and Mama both insisted we
needed an education. I walked three or four miles most days
to catch a milk truck the rest of the way into town to go, because that was what he expected. And I loved school and
loved my teachers. Papa only got to the sixth grade himself,
but people out our way called him Professor Massengale. He
was the only one in the community who could read. He'd sit
out on Sunday reading the newspaper aloud and explaining it
to the old folks. They'd come by our house, twenty five, thirty
people sitting around on our porch. He'd wait until they all
got there and then read the paper, telling them what was
going on in the world. In meetings at the old Community
Center, people would wait for him—'We want Hugh here,'
they said. He had their respect. I never forgot the impression
that made on me.

"I remember him standing there in the Church of Christ
choir. He was a devout member, as I am. I can see him, singing
in a clean khaki work suit and shined shoes, very neat. He
couldn't afford a business suit but he was meticulous—he had
nothing, but he had *something*, you know?"

MOST OF the places the Massengales lived were outside Marshall in a little settlement called Crossroads, out where Farm Roads 31, 2625 and 2199 intersect. This level land is still rich for farming and logging. The houses out here were spaced wide apart and the fields provided a living for the Massengale family.

Bonnie Parker and Clyde Barrow knew these back roads well. Their crime spree covered the countryside between Missouri and Louisiana during Joe's first five years. They were known to buy shelter for the night from the needy people in Crossroads for whom ten or twenty dollars was a fortune; it was a place, as Bonnie's famous autobiographical poem put it, "Where the women are kin, / And the men are men, / And they won't 'stool' on Bonnie and Clyde." The robbers stole one of their favorite cars from a man in Marshall—one morning, Robert Rosborough found that his convertible was missing from his driveway. Bonnie and Clyde posed with the car in snapshots, cigars and guns in hand, and put 3,000 miles on it before Rosborough got it back.

Growing up here, Joe learned quickly learned about what confidence was and what it was not. His life depended on it.

"I must have been about eight years old," he remembers, "when a Black man, Bakey Makum, lived near us out on Acie Rhodes Road. He worked for a couple of White women. People would see them driving into town side by side in a two-seater for the store they ran. My dad told him one day, 'Bakey, don't be driving with those women sitting up so close to you.' Bakey said, 'Mister Hugh, ain't nothing happening between us,' but one of the women got pregnant. Some of the White men went down and told Bakey to meet them the next morning. They said, 'Bakey, you're gonna die this morning,' and they shot him. He tried to run. He fell, got up, kept running. People were yelling from their porches, *'Run, Bakey!'* and he's running down the road, they're shooting, and the women are yelling, *'Run, run hard as you can!'* He dropped. They put a chain around him, dragged him all the way down the highway and back, right by our house. It was all over town what happened. No one got arrested for that. No one got arrested the night a White man's wagon hit ours out on the road and the baby we called Little Brother was killed. The man who hit us said, 'Niggers shouldn't be driving no wagon at night.' We had to live with that.

"That's the difference—confidence isn't foolishness. You had to learn that. You had to be confident to stay alive, but you had to understand what confidence meant. If you were foolish, you'd pay. Your whole family would pay. Bakey Makum had seven children.

"It was hard to keep that in mind sometimes, and people forgot. It could easily have happened to my father or to me. It used to happen that our mules would get out and wander on up to Mister John's place. He had good feed and water, and he fed our mules knowing they'd get out and go up there. He charged my dad three dollars to get them back. My dad paid it once but he knew what Mister John was doing—he was deliberately attracting those mules so he could take the money. They went up again and Mister John told someone, 'Hey, you tell that nigger his mules is here.' He wanted to get four dollars from my dad for it, and my dad didn't get the money—he got his rifle. Mama was just screaming, but Dad said, 'I'm going to get my mules this morning.' One of my brothers went to get a neighbor to stop him. My dad was limping up the road with his gun and the neighbor stood in the road with his arms out and said, 'Hugh, don't do this. I'll pay for them.' My dad said, 'No, I'm gonna kill him'—man, when he got angry it was something. I got a lot of that temper but I stay away from those feelings unless someone's trying to take advantage of me. I don't let that happen. You can't live the way we did in Texas and not get angry. There was always that fine line. People back then would do anything to rob you of your confidence and self-respect, in a thousand little ways, every day. But you couldn't lose your temper. That would get you killed.

"My dad made a better choice that day he went after his mules," he says. "It saved his life. It's a dangerous thing, being angry . . . some people never get over their anger. I've shown mine at times I shouldn't have. But I grew bigger than that. I *had* to grow bigger. There's been so many times when I might have said something or done something, but instead I just left it alone. Some people make it their whole lives, just being angry. But if you had a mind to do something in life, you just couldn't mess up and lose it all in a moment of feeling that way. I took what I saw in Marshall, took what my dad expected of me, and I made those things useful for myself.

"I didn't deny the truth about what happened. I didn't forget it. I thought about it. And I used it to make me more confident."

▦

JOE LEAFS through the clippings from *The Marshall News-Messenger* about his Hall of Fame induction. The front-page story shows Joe with the president of Wiley College beside a story titled "Horse Sense: Marshall Native Returns Home to Be Honored."

"Everything I learned in Marshall works for me now, not against me," Joe says. "I've been landscaping for sixty years, and tell people all the time, I'm number one in Los Angeles. My company, Joe's Expert Tree Service, gets the most referrals and the most repeat business. I don't like being number two. I was always like that. But I don't take success for granted. I earn it, like I earned it back home. I set a standard and my customers know that they can be confident in me to keep it. It shows in my company's work, and in how we conduct ourselves. That's why my customers call us back. I got that attitude in Marshall. That was the first thing my father gave to me: I could *choose* how I felt. I could choose and I could always feel confident that I could do better."

The *News-Messenger* story tells of the Massengale family's return for the celebration. Joe's sons got a chance to convey their honor for their father; moreover, Joe got to thank Marshall for what it had given him. Someone else might have seen the moment as an opportunity to express a break with the past, but for the Massengales, the welcome was genuine; so was the gratitude they expressed.

"To go to Marshall today," Joe says, "you wouldn't believe any of the bad times ever happened. When I went back, it was, 'Yes, sir!' The policemen in front of the Courthouse said that to me on the same spot where my father was almost killed, where I used to get run off trying to hustle a nickel for a shoeshine."

Joe serves lunch, plates of steaming catfish, potatoes and

greens he grows himself, while he reminisces today. He always says grace.

"Good things happen. You can choose to make them happen. There are so many good people you meet, and if they see goodness in you, they give you back their own. A friend and I went from Marshall to Houston in about '45. I was sixteen. My shoes were old, and my mother cut me out some cardboard insoles to put in them so I could walk around looking for a job. We left the day after high school closed for the summer. I had four dollars to take me two hundred miles. We were carrying some extra clothes and a sandwich, and that was it. We had no place to sleep. I remember walking around Houston, probably looking lost. This old Black man observed us. He said, 'You boys live around here?' We said, 'No, we're from Marshall, we're here hoping to find jobs.' He said, 'Where you going, you got friends?' We said, 'No, we thought we'd just stay mostly anywhere.' He said, 'Come on with me.' That man fixed us dinner and gave us a place to sleep. I guess he could see we were good boys. My friend got a job next morning shining shoes and I got a job at the Alabama Café busing tables. Well, that went fine until one day I came out from the kitchen and a man was disrespecting one of the waitresses, and I objected. I led thirty workers out of that place. I didn't want to stay there if we weren't going to be respected. This was right in the middle of lunch. I just led everybody out, the whole staff. People were saying, 'You're all gonna listen to this young squirt, sixteen years old, telling you to walk out?' They did. I caught the bus and went home to Marshall. The sad thing is, every one of them went back except me. I don't go back. Proverbs 26, remember? 'As a dog returns to its vomit, so a fool repeats his folly.' You need to have the confidence it takes to be right and stay right even when it means making a sacrifice. My dad showed me that. He didn't make trouble but he didn't back down."

Joe serves seconds and leafs through the clippings and the flyers about Marshall.

"I went back to Houston in '46 because I'd heard some people talking about construction jobs. They said, 'Just show up and you have a chance.' I was right there when they were calling out names, and they called out every name but mine until an old Black gentleman there, Mister Howard, said to me, 'Son, what's your daddy's name?' I said, 'My daddy is Hugh Massengale.' "

Joe's eyes mist over and he has to take a long pause before he continues the story. "This is rough for me to say," he admits.

"Mister Howard said, 'Boy, Hugh Massengale is your daddy?' He turned right there to the foreman and said, 'Hire this boy. If he's Hugh Massengale's son, he'll work.' Made me proud to know people thought of my father that way. It still does."

Sixty years after losing his father, Joe still needs to pause when he is asked if he and his father were close.

"Just being in his company, that was close. He talked more to my older brothers, I imagine. When they left for California, I was the oldest one at home, and then he'd talk to me a little more. He didn't talk to us a lot about things he felt we needed to know. He knew us so well, he didn't need to be too heavy on the instructions. He knew we were going to be good men and women.

"I don't remember particular conversations except when he was dying. My mother told me, You know your dad isn't going to be with us too long. And I asked him. He said, 'Oh no, son, I'm all right.' Very strong man. He knew he was going, dying of cancer. He didn't want anyone upset. He passed not long after that.

"The day he died, I was shining shoes at the barbershop of the Marshall Hotel on Courthouse Square—that was a step up from shining on the street. The phone rang and the barber told me, 'Shine, you better go on home.' The man in the chair asked about it, and the barber said, 'That boy's daddy just died. Hugh Massengale.' Man in the chair sat up and said, 'Hugh Massengale? Well, we lost a good nigger.'"

It is 1,885 miles by rail from Marshall to Los Angeles. At sixteen, when Joe first asked, he was told that the price of a one-way ticket was $40.20. "Oh, my goodness!" he said to the man at the Texas and Pacific station on Washington Street. It seemed like a fortune to the kid who earned his money shining shoes for nickels.

"That'll keep you here, won't it," growled the man behind the counter.

Joe was on the next day's train out.

■■■

"THAT WAS 1945 . . . the same year I came to California," he says. "My brothers were here, and I lived with them and got a job at a produce warehouse. I used to wash the owner's Cadillacs. Nice fellow. Well, towards the end of the summer I told him I would be leaving to go back to Texas to finish high school. He said to me, 'You know how they treat you down there, why do you want to go back? You're a smart man, you're making friends here, you have a future here.' He took me to his home. Beautiful place. Met his wife, had a nice lunch. He said, 'This is the way you're supposed to be living. Why do you want to go back?' I'll tell you, that man put me to thinking. I really did want to go back to Texas to finish school, but I remembered what he told me. And when I got back to Marshall, my ideas were different. I'd seen how it could be. And what that man said to me raised my expectations. I could make a better choice. He raised my confidence."

Joe pauses a moment to get the plaque that shows clients that Joe's Expert Tree Service belongs to the Better Business Bureau in Los Angeles. It means as much to him as the racing trophies in his study.

"I started my business here in 1947, door-to-door. I didn't have a dime. My partner and I would go up and down the streets, him on one side and me on the other, knowing that we had to pay for the rented truck and a place to sleep that night. If there was ever a time that tested my confidence, that was it.

"But I had what I learned in Marshall: confidence is watching and trusting yourself, but not assuming. It's being honest and keeping your word, not taking something that isn't yours. It's not so hard, is it? It seems obvious, but I see executives in corporations who still don't get it. They act like confidence is bluffing somebody. They're foolish. My clients live in Palm Springs and Beverly Hills—they're smart people, and you can't bluff someone who's smart. I wouldn't try to. They see my work. It's all right there. I respect them and they respect me for what I know.

"Want to know the difference that makes for the people I

sell to? I can be driving by a person's house and look at a tree in their yard. I can tell if it's overgrown and top heavy. It might look beautiful, all thick leaves and green up there, but if it's too dense at the top for the trunk to carry it, and those Santa Ana winds come or the rain gets at it, that tree will be lying across the driveway.

"It's part of my job to explain that to the owner of the house. Chances are, that's someone who's never seen me before, someone who has no idea who I am, and it might be someone who's had a bad experience with a contractor. So this person's skeptical. I have to be confident enough in myself and what I know to give them confidence in me. So when I knock on someone's door, I'm on their property and I look like I'm there to perform a service. I'm wearing a clean uniform, paying attention; I'm speaking with courtesy and making eye contact; asking direct questions and giving straight answers. That gives a good impression. It's how you earn someone's trust. Neatness means a lot. Confidence is what it gives you. 'Good morning, sir,' I say. 'How are you today? In passing by this morning I noticed this beautiful tree you have, and I can see that it's a bit too heavy for its trunk. Look at the size of the branches, the base, and look how heavy it is up top. Now, suppose there come up a wind, forty-five, fifty miles an hour, and it breaks a big limb. You might as well take the whole thing down if that happens. Would you rather make some cuts now, or else wait and take a chance?'

"It happens all the time that they say no, and I leave my card with them and wish them well. And the winds do come up. And that tree might be one of dozens, hundreds, that get knocked down by the Santa Anas every year here in California. And they call me in the middle of the night to get it out of their way.

"My boys and I did all kinds of emergency work like that. And people said to me, 'You prophesied this tree coming down! How did you know?' I just say, 'No, I could see it was too heavy, that's all.' It might take me all day to remove that tree, and I charge a premium for emergency work. People tell me I'm a good salesman, but really all I do is tell the truth. That's why my customers stay with me for years, decades even. I tell the truth, and I do good work. That's what inspires their confidence.

"I love America for that, let me tell you. Tell the truth, do what you say you'll do, and you'll do all right. Somebody says something about not getting ahead in this country, I'm going to correct them. Of course there's been injustice, we know that. It's done and we won't forget it. But if all you do is dwell on it, you can't make any progress. You're finished if you let it be finished there. It's a choice. Yes, you get knocked down. Don't stay there. That's not the Massengale way. My dad taught me that and I taught that to my sons. There's enough here for all of us. Just believe in yourself and make a better choice."

We had to be confident of ourselves. Not arrogant; not difficult. But confident that we were as good as anyone and had the same right as anyone had to be here and to work hard.

JOE MASSENGALE, JR., the eldest of Joe's six sons, is a real estate agent and mortgage broker in Philadelphia. His business letterhead is Galatians 6:10: *And as we have therefore opportunity, let us do good unto all men, especially unto them who are of the household of faith.*

Joe Jr. looks like his father, with the same salt-and-pepper mustache. He does most of his business in his car, scouting the Victorian rowhouses and duplexes in West Philadelphia and the stone and brick homes in the suburbs of the city. He prefers to do it personally rather than sell using only a listing. In a typical week he'll look at ten or fifteen houses, all with a specific customer in mind.

Today he's coming straight off the red-eye flight from San Francisco, where he visited one of his children, a student at Stanford University. It's the day after a heavy snow, and most of the city schools and offices are closed. The trees are white and the roads slippery as Joe Jr. picks up his car at the airport and visits three properties before going home. When he finally gets there, the cell phone, his desk line and the fax machine are humming.

His office is a small, cluttered paneled room attached to his house, with family pictures and a banner from Isaiah 54:17 on the wall: "No weapon formed against me shall prosper."

Joe Jr.'s trip to Marshall with his father for the Hall of Fame induction was the first time he'd been back since boyhood. "I began to understand my father better when we went back to Texas," he says. "Of course I'd heard his stories about where he grew up, but getting a chance to see it—to really feel it—no story can capture that. Visiting the graves of my mother's parents, going to my paternal grandfather's grave ... my dad pointed to a spot and told us, 'That was my house'—and there was nothing there but trees. You can't capture those feelings secondhand.

"I wanted to go back again because I think it's necessary for all of us in my family, regardless of where we are, to be connected to Marshall, and to find out as much as possible about where we came from. What makes my dad's story important to me isn't what he has now. It's how he survived, how he came from a place where he had nothing and never permitted himself to feel discouraged. He's never lived any other way. We took all that for granted, my brothers and I. We were certainly protected from the things he knew, hunger and physical need, because he gave us everything we could possibly want. So I don't think we understood his background. Growing up in Los Angeles, we didn't know. In Texas, I could *feel* the story about his father dying. I could feel the way it must have been, the sheer weight of the past in Courthouse Square where he was a shoeshine boy ... I could *feel* all those things.

"I think he lived a quintessential American story. There are lots of people who have stories of greater success, but my dad's story is one of going from absolutely nothing, with no way of getting ahead, to a man who is seventy-seven and healthy and happy with his family. He's an extraordinary guy."

Is there a single key idea Joe Jr. learned from his father? He doesn't hesitate. "Confidence," he says.

"I use the confidence he taught me every day in what I do for a living and in my family life. I started working for my father when I was five—and I tried going to work with him when I was three! By age eight, I was a veteran on the landscaping crew. I bought my own uniform when I was ten. And I saw the police officers chasing us off, the skeptical neighbors asking our customers, 'Why are you paying those Black boys so much for yard work?' Black men working in White neighborhoods in the 1960s, the 1970s, going out every day and *making the business happen*—we *had* to be confident of ourselves. Not bigheaded. Not difficult. But confident that we were as good as anyone and had the same right as anyone to be there and to work hard.

"A lot of people would have been afraid to do that. But we were told what to expect. My dad explained it to us step-by-step: you're in Beverly Hills, Palm Springs. *Pay attention.* As you're going up to the door, there will be people watching you from the windows, eyes watching from across the street. The police will come and ask us what we're doing here. I was ten, eleven years old, and I had a script memorized, 'Good morning, Officer, how are you? That's right, we're here working for Mrs. So-and-so and . . .' We all knew what to say.

"It could get confrontational sometimes, but I was the

eldest brother, and it was my job to not lose my temper. I wanted to be smooth, calm, easy to get along with. Not deferential; just a gentleman doing his job. I don't lose my temper, and confidence is the key to it. I just stay calm. I'm confident things are going to work out."

The phones and e-mails don't keep Joe Jr. from telling his story. The story doesn't keep him from doing business.

"My dad taught us by example," he continues. "We worked for a lot of movie stars, for one thing. Famous people, people used to attention. It was drilled into me from day one that I was just as good as they were. One time my brother asked a famous actor for his autograph. Nice guy really, and my brother was excited. My dad said, 'Don't you ever ask anyone for an autograph. They should be excited meeting *you*.' We learned to think, 'Hey, so and so met a Massengale today.'

"More than that, he taught us to believe the work would be there if we asked for it. That takes a lot of confidence, believe me, getting up every day not knowing where or if there would be a job at all. But he had that rock-solid faith in himself and dared to ask for it, and to teach us to ask, and to keep asking, not out of some kind of feeling that we were entitled, but because we knew we could keep the promises we made. We could ask for challenges because we were equal to them. He never got discouraged. He didn't let us get that way. We'd be out on the road for days, driving all over Southern California, and we'd come to the place on the highway where you could turn south to San Diego or north toward home, and he'd ask me, 'How much money do you have in your pocket?' 'Sixty, seventy dollars,' I'd tell him. 'Not enough,' he'd say, and we'd all turn south. If that's where the work was, that's where we'd go.

That's the lesson here. Nothing happens unless you go after it with confidence."

Joe Jr. spends a couple of hours catching up with messages and clients, splitting the time equally between work calls and calls to his friends at church and in the neighborhood. The first thing he did when he got home today was shovel his own driveway and sidewalk. Then he did the same for the couple next door. Now he heads back to the car.

"I had some great teachers in college and grad school. But the fact is, I can't remember one professor or one class that gave me this understanding. It came from watching my dad in the truck, driving up and down the street, walking up those front walks and asking for jobs: head up, be polite, make eye contact. I've always felt comfortable talking with people, one-to-one or in a group, and that's where it comes from. That ability gave our customers confidence then, and it works in my business now.

"People called my dad 'Boss,' even his older brothers. He was always the one among his brothers who led, even though he wasn't the eldest. They'd get involved in big landscaping jobs when he first came out to California, and the others might say, 'Boss, we can't do this,' and he'd say, 'The "can't" word isn't in my vocabulary.' He *lived* his confidence. He worked as though everything was going to be okay even when it wasn't. I think about that all the time in my life now—I have pressures, demanding clients, lots of things happening; people and circumstances constantly telling me 'no.' I just keep going as if 'no' doesn't apply, and if plan A doesn't work, I go to plan B, plan C, plan D. You keep going, use alternatives, check what you missed, and adjust. *Forward motion.*"

Joe Jr. laughs, remembering. "We were a *machine* on the trees. We listened, we executed. My dad had a great sense of salesmanship. He'd tell the client, 'Okay, Mr. Jones, we're gonna go to work.' By that time, of course, the ladder was up in the tree and my brother Michael and I were already cutting. It was timed, choreographed. My dad has that sense of style. And man, we moved fast and thought fast and performed fast. We had to pay attention all the time. My dad knew it was all about the way you took your place, the way you conducted yourself. Be confident you can do your job, earn what you get, and deliver every time. Same when I went to college. I was with a student body that was almost entirely White. African-American students can psych themselves out in a setting like that—I didn't. I knew who I was, and I knew I deserved to be there."

Joe Jr.'s cell phone rings repeatedly as he drives. He takes every call.

WEST PHILADELPHIA, the territory where Joe serves his first-time home buyers, includes the upscale stores, galleries, classrooms, dorms, museums and laboratories around Drexel University, the Philadelphia University of the Sciences and the University of Pennsylvania, and also some of the city's most depressed neighborhoods.

The area is rich in history. Satterlee Hospital stood at 44th Street and Baltimore Avenue. It was the second-largest in the nation when it treated the wounded from the Battle of Gettysburg. Bartram's Garden, the nation's first botanical garden, where Benjamin Franklin visited his friend John Bartram, still hugs the bank of the Schuylkill River. West Philly includes Philadelphia's enormous Fairmount Park. Some remnants of the 1876 Centennial Exhibition survive in Parkside, across the street from rows of deteriorated but stately Gilded Age houses built at the time when West Philly was a country retreat from the heart of the city. On what are now broad green lawns were enormous pavilions with thirteen acres of new inventions and gadgets. Galvanized steel cables, the typewriter, and Alexander Graham Bell's telephone were introduced here to an amazed public. Powering all the mechanical exhibits was the colossal Corliss Engine, driving five miles of shafts to run the amazing new devices, including a high-speed lumber cutter performing with steam power the work Hugh Massengale did for a living by hand in Texas.

Most of the Exhibition buildings were temporary and have long since vanished, but the great granite Memorial Hall still stands, topped by a statue of Columbia bearing a laurel branch of glory. President Ulysses S. Grant was present in Memorial Hall to open the fair in 1876. It was the year *Tom Sawyer* was published, and the year Custer died at Little Big Horn, twelve years before Joe Jr.'s grandfather Hugh was born.

Among the exhibits at the Centennial was a statue of a joyous freed slave wearing broken shackles.

For all the progress on display at the Exhibition, the age when this part of Philadelphia flourished was a time of terrible setbacks for African-Americans. President Grant's efforts to enforce Reconstruction in the reunited nation were mostly abandoned after the compromise Hayes-Tilden election of 1876. The Civil Rights Act of 1875, an attempt to guarantee

universal social rights such as full and equal access to accom-
modation in hotels, public conveyance and theaters, was de-
clared unconstitutional by the Supreme Court in 1883, when
the Court asserted that Congress did not have the power to
regulate the conduct and transactions of individuals. It was
the last attempt by Congress to protect the civil rights of African-
Americans until the mid–twentieth century, and the Court's
ruling opened an era of legalized discrimination and sanc-
tioned separation between Whites and Blacks in the United
States. During the Jim Crow era in America, the shackles may
as well have been back on.

Hugh Massengale was born in this time, and almost died
in it. Joe Massengale lived with the shadow of Jim Crow during his boyhood. When the houses Joe Massengale, Jr., sells
today were built, African-Americans were not allowed to
buy them.

FOR A real estate broker or a builder, West Philly is hot territory. The big schools near here create huge demand for houses
and apartments. Prices have skyrocketed for any house, no
matter how poor the condition.

Joe Jr. heads for a property near the University of Pennsylvania to meet an owner who wants to sell and a prospective buyer. At 46th and Locust Streets, he parks in front of
a derelict rowhouse, one of thousands in the city. Typically,
these late-nineteenth- and early-twentieth-century houses are
three or four stories tall, and still handsome on the outside
with copper drainpipes, stone facades and leaded glass win-

dows. This one has plywood in the window. The owner needs a crowbar to get in.

The inside is a dark, dangerous wreck, with water coming in gaping holes in the ceiling. The floors and walls groan and buckle. Ruined furniture and trash fill the icy rooms. Joe and the buyer walk carefully with flashlights assessing the time and cost of repairing the place.

"Oh, man," says the buyer, shining his light up. "Look at this." Sunlight comes in from overhead, and melting snow drips down into the living room. The hole in the ceiling is a yard wide. He leads Joe Jr. along a gloomy corridor toward the back. More melting snow puddles in the bathroom. The bedrooms are just as bad. The kitchen floor creaks as they walk.

It's worse downstairs and in the basement. "This one's totaled," says the buyer. "It'll need to be gutted to the studs. I'm looking at a year of work. Ten grand just to clean it out." It's hard to believe that the seller wants nearly two hundred thousand dollars for the building, but then again, it's within walking distance of the Penn campus, and still solid enough that next year this ruin could be two modern two-bedroom apartments with four-figure rents and a view of downtown Philly.

Joe Jr. loves the idea of raising this home from the dead. "You need a five-year vision to make money in real estate," he says, "and Philadelphia is one of the places where smart buyers can still do well. This neighborhood has dozens of places even worse than this. The walls here are sound. Under all that destruction and neglect, everything you need to work with is still there. It'll be a real pleasure watching that house come back to life."

BACK IN the car, the phone rings again. "I really pay attention to phone calls," Joe says. "People reach me no matter where I am, here, on vacation, wherever. I work by myself, and I work fast; it's hard for me to find associates who can move at the pace I want to keep. I found the last three or four houses my clients bought. I find a place I know is right for them and call them, and say, 'I've got your house. I'm standing in your living room. Tell your husband I'm going to pick him up.' He comes, he stands there and calls her—'Honey, stop what you're doing. Joe's coming back to get you.' I go pick up the wife. They're together in their home for the first time, and I'm there with them. That's an incredible feeling."

Joe's telephone flashes numbers in his hand: "I get instant notices on interest rates and bonds constantly," he explains. "I say a prayer every time that I can get my clients the most favorable rate—rates change in a flash and I have to make a choice. I get on the phone, call the company I do business with, commit to a rate and say a prayer. That takes confidence too—you need to commit. You can't wait around hoping for something better."

Another call comes. This client is a young single mother who hopes to buy a house in the Overbrook Park area, the neighborhood where astronaut Guy Bluford and basketball legend Wilt Chamberlain grew up. This wouldn't be the most desirable sale for a bigger realtor, and the commission at the end for Joe Jr. won't be the biggest he'll get this month, but he makes a special effort for this buyer, knowing the difference it will make for her and her child to be in their own home. This is a scary step for the buyer, but Joe Jr. asks her to stretch—"I want you to expand your horizons a little," he tells her. "It's time you stopped being a renter and became an investor. You can do this. I'll be right there with you."

He smiles when the call is over. "People ask me all the time to get them 'something cheap in a nice neighborhood.' I have to tell them, 'Hey, nice and cheap don't come in the same sentence in this market.' But you can still get something good here if you're smart and willing to push yourself a little. I want to see this woman with a roof of her own over her head, and I'll do what it takes to make that happen."

The phone rings again. "Every call I take is important to me," he says when he's off. "I'm getting back to service as a personal commitment in a way it was missing from my life when I was practicing law. For a client who calls me with an inquiry, I'll prepare a credit report. It's a way to diagnose someone's financial strengths and weaknesses. I write a cover letter with it. No charge for that. This woman in Overbrook Park needs some help because she's young and single and a parent. I need to be creative on her behalf. I can give her some goals to work on and set up a time to talk, and that's all free. She'll know what her prospects are; she'll know the things she needs to do to get her affairs in order and be a responsible owner. And she's a friend now, not just a client. My commitment to her is personal. That's my mission. That's why my company is called Spirit Financial Group. That comes from my personal relationship with God, and that's helped me more than I can say. It helped me through the end of my first marriage, helped me through everything it took to start over and build my business."

Anyone might see how ambitious Joe Massengale, Jr., is—a one-man operation seeking to make a difference in people's lives, driving to houses all over the city by himself. Is that overconfidence?

Joe Jr. smiles. "My dad taught me that there's a difference between confidence and arrogance," Joe says. "Arrogance is not paying attention, thinking you're invulnerable. Where he grew up, not understanding that distinction could get you killed. When I grew up, if you were too confident in our land-scaping and tree business, you'd get hurt or arrested or you'd lose the customer. But really, if you're arrogant anywhere, you'll be in trouble—your business, your marriage, doesn't matter. Race has nothing to do with it. Arrogance hurts you no matter who you are, and I know it firsthand. The other half of being confident enough to build something is being hum-ble enough to know how fast you can lose it. Growing up in Los Angeles, we saw it happen all the time. Athletes, enter-tainers, people we knew hit the top then lost everything. My dad emphasized to me that nobody's invulnerable, that even people at the peak can lose it all if they aren't careful. He never let us forget that.

"My brothers and me: six African-American boys, a single-parent household, a major American city, in that time . . . by the statistics, we were the most vulnerable people of all to drugs or crime. How many boys in that position never sur-vived to become men? How many are in trouble now? We didn't let it touch us. We couldn't. People have asked me, 'How did you escape what happened to so many other people?' I always say, 'My father.' He had us believing that people who used drugs, people who got into trouble, couldn't be as tidy as we were, couldn't live in a nice house like we did, wouldn't be respected in church—and he was clear about it, that we were better than that, and it would shame the family if we forgot it. Our name meant something to him. It was my name too, and I had to invest myself in keeping it honorable. If I was arrogant or foolish about it, that was a mistake. If I was confident, I watched and worked to make that name mean something positive."

THE PHILADELPHIA skyline stands tall in the distance as Joe Jr. heads west back toward the city line.

"Today I'm a licensed mortgage broker and real estate agent," he says. "It's not where I started. I went to law school in Los Angeles and practiced for a while, and when my first wife and I moved to Philadelphia, I worked as a stockbroker and bond broker. I left that to do automotive leasing and provide financing for people buying cars and equipment. Then I started my own company.

"My marriage had ended. I was looking for a better purpose in my life. I *needed* it. My own maturity was the missing element. In my first marriage, my former wife and I were both attorneys, and I was just too attentive to the money and the career and the aura of it. We socialized all the time with our professional peers, lawyers and judges. I remember talking about fees and cases and the work . . . and not one time was there a conversation about the heart, the soul, about what we're here on earth to do with our lives, or about what mattered to us beyond the new car and the vacation house.

"Money can't fill that emptiness you feel when you have arrogance but not confidence. Confidence is deeper than that. It's a feeling of purpose in your heart.

"My confidence now is different from what it was then. Maybe that's the paradox of it—I'm more humble now, humble enough to serve a bigger purpose, and I feel more confident because of that. When your heart is at peace, really at peace, there's nothing you can't do. I get up and walk three miles every morning, like my dad. Got my earphones on, listening to a sermon or Christian music and I just thank God and say, *Man, this is a good day to be alive*. After that, everything gets easier.

"My wife Pat went to college in West Philadelphia. Wharton School of Business, Class of 1980. She and her family have been a tremendous influence on my personal spirituality. We met in 1991. Her children were playing soccer with mine. We'd never seen each other, and that first time we talked, she said three things to me I'll never forget. She said one, she wouldn't date a faithless man. Two, she attended Christian Stronghold Baptist Church, and her whole family was active in it. And three, she asked me then and there, what are your intentions? Heavy stuff for a casual conversation on the playground. It changed my life.

"My focus today is better than it used to be. Before I relied on myself. Today I'd say my relationship with God is the essence of my confidence. I think my dad's was essential to his confidence as he became a man back in Texas. His father, Hugh, was an active churchgoer. The Church of Christ had missionaries going around to places like Crossroads helping Black folks learn how to read. Hugh and Susie used to give the missionaries a place to stay for the night. They had next to nothing themselves, but they fed and sheltered those folks. They talked and listened and their kids learned. I think those people helped Hugh and people like him appreciate what it meant to learn and advance. It was uplifting, showing them that they could transform their lives.

"So I'm not so much confident in myself; I'm confident in something far greater. I'm blessed. God's giving me the means to do something with my life. My understanding of this has become much clearer as I've grown older, and I think that I enjoy this time more than any other time in my life—I have a sense of purpose beyond anything I had before.

"My business has taken off, and it's because service is first for me. That's where I'm dedicated to doing a good job. Not adequate, not acceptable. *Better* than that. I want to be confident enough to meet my own standards, the ones my clients don't know I set. My dad's known for doing that kind of job. I got that from him. At seventy-seven Joe Sr. still goes around to his customers' houses even when they aren't there and looks over their property to see that it meets his standards." Joe laughs, remembering. "I remember once, we were working for someone in a beautiful home and my head was someplace else. My dad said to me, 'Joe, you're leaving leaves everywhere. These people don't hire me to make the flowerbeds look like that.' Right then the owner comes back and tells us, 'Fellas, it doesn't have to be perfect.' My dad told her, 'Ma'am, it has to be perfect for *me*.' I had that flowerbed looking like a swept floor. I mean, *immaculate*. That sort of thing happened many times. And man, that's a lesson to keep in mind if you do business.

"Look at companies today—how many businesses set a

higher standard? How many companies just get away with doing as little as what the customer will accept? My business only got better when I put my father's lesson about confidence to work. Arrogance is taking. Confidence is giving. Now I give to my customers, and my whole life is better for it."

Joe Jr. stops at home to eat quickly before heading back to West Philadelphia again for Wednesday-night Bible study. Christian Stronghold Baptist Church is built in a converted supermarket not far from Overbrook High School. The place hums with classrooms, meeting areas and a fifteen-hundred-seat auditorium that fills for services three times every Sunday.

Joe Jr. is everywhere, greeting people, stopping by meetings and shaking hands until the study session starts. He sits with a Bible open on one knee and a notepad on the other. The Book of Joel is the focus tonight. The lesson is about priorities. People stand and testify about what matters in their lives, and about moments when they put the wrong things first.

Before he leaves, Joe Jr. makes sure to talk quietly with a couple of friends. "I can do all things in my life through God who strengthens me," he says on the way home. "I don't need to be confident alone. I know He feels confidence in me.

"My wife and I feel the same way about this. When you look at yourself as a catalyst, you know your words are important. You must walk that confidence, and know what it does to the lives around you. You're capable of things you don't even know, both good and bad. People see you, how you conduct yourself, how you relate to them. An older lady at church once told me that she appreciated how I treat my wife, how I show her respect and affection. I had no idea she was observing me, and that reminded me that we're being seen all the time, all of us.

"We have five children. Our eldest daughter is thirty. Our second eldest is at Stanford. We have a son in the Navy, another son at college in Carlisle and another at Shippensburg University. People look at my family, my brothers around the country, and my family here, and they say we've achieved a lot. That's good and fine, but material achievement really is secondary. What's primary is the strength inside that comes with confidence. We need that today in African-American families and businesses. We need to be emphasizing manhood and fatherhood and responsibility, so we can give the best of ourselves."

A successful niche player in a market with a substantial African-American population would bring a lot to a citywide company or even a national realtor. Would Joe Jr. consider taking a position with one of his bigger competitors? He laughs—"I was offered a chance recently to go to a large firm. They wanted me just for the real estate and wouldn't let me do the mortgages, though, and more important . . . they wouldn't let me *say* what I say now. I wouldn't be able to work the way I work. Big companies sometimes emphasize service but they don't *live* service. They couldn't do the deals I do— I meet other people in the business who just want to get it done, get the money, always talking about *me, me, me,* and I think, Wait a minute, isn't this about the *client*?"

He brings up the passage from Galatians on his company letterhead. "Working by myself is harder, but it means I can be both a mortgage broker and a real estate agent. If I gave one role up I couldn't be as flexible as I am now, especially with my first-time home buyers. And I don't think a big outfit would get my mission statement, *Let us do good unto all men*. It might make me eccentric or strange in their eyes, and I can understand that. Keep in mind, it's no sacrifice to me to work alone. I think I can put two hundred buyers in two hundred houses next year. But I have a personal relationship with my clients that a big company might not permit me to have. That's even more rewarding, and too important to me to give up. I wouldn't want to change the way I do business, because my business is giving, and I get back tenfold with that in mind.

"And you know, bigger opportunities are happening. Maybe it's my dad's confidence coming through again, because some of the business I'm doing is new to me, but my dad never said no when clients asked him to try something he'd never done before. I'm breaking in to circles I never worked in before, for amounts bigger than I ever dealt with, and I'm finding that they like what I have to offer them. Luke 19 . . . *Because you have been trustworthy in a very small matter, take charge of ten cities*. It's true.

"Look at my brothers and me—not one of us works a typical nine-to-five job. Why? We all learned that we had what we needed to survive, that our independence didn't need to be sacrificed for us to live the lives we wanted to live. My dad had his failures and we saw them all. But he kept going. He showed us we could too. You can't have the attitude of giving up. I tell that to my kids all the time: even when the door looks like it's locked, try it anyway. Just try. That's what my father taught me. Just give your best effort. Give the best you have, and be confident that good things will happen. That's my attitude. That's where I'm from."

LESSON TWO

FORTITUDE

Preface by Anjelica Huston

An actor's dream: opening night in the role of a lifetime before a New York audience. My grandfather's dream came true the night in 1937 he brought his Othello to the Amsterdam Theatre.

Walter Huston was fifty-three years old. He started acting at eighteen in Canada, and spent his early years in the provinces and in the American Midwest, doing song-and-dance vaudeville and any little role he could get in repertory companies, wearing homemade costumes and hoping to find a place to sleep in towns where actors were not welcome. For some years he left the stage—John Huston, my father, was born when Walter was managing a power-and-light company in Nevada, Missouri—but it drew him back. He willed himself to be an actor.

Shakespeare was the peak, the riskiest, most challenging, richest work an actor could hope to do, and Walter had built his Othello with years of practice. He also had a six-figure cash investment in the production. When the curtain went up that night, all the work he'd put into the role and all the years before that in all the little halls and theaters paid off—he thought. He remarked to his colleagues during the play how well he knew it was going, and how much the audience liked it. "We sailed in and played Othello with a relish and a zest, played it as we would have on a dare—with all the knowledge we had, with all the verve and *understanding we could bring to it," he said later. "We earnestly believed, as deep down as a man can, that we had given a hell of a performance, as fine a piece of work as our lives ever fashioned . . ."*

That night he stayed up to get the early editions of the newspapers and see the reviews he felt certain would be glowing. They weren't. The praise was faint at best— "One came away with a sense more of spectacle than of drama"—and damning at worst. They singled Walter out for particular criticism: "sluggish," he was, and "casual."

Walter was devastated. He adapted his performance to try to achieve what the reviewers and the audiences felt Othello ought to be. He played it more frenetic, louder and wilder, and disturbed his fellow actors with this new approach. It only made things worse. "Any twenty-year-old schoolboy could have played it that way," he said. "If that is acting, I have spent the last twenty-five years in vain."

My grandfather said it was his first failure in thirteen years, but I suspect that can't be true. No one goes that long without failing. In fact, he must have felt he'd failed at hundreds of performances before this one, and perhaps even at his whole attempt to be an actor. But he had come to terms with failure, and even understood its value. Failure "balances the books," he said. "It draws you up sharp and makes you take stock." It reminded him of the need to stay strong, to take the risks, to assume nothing and to pay attention always, always, because no success is inevitable. You must earn it, and if you earn this one, you still need to earn your next one too. "I'm glad I was a failure," he said, "or I should have forgotten these simple things, things I learned many years ago, when, wandering about the streets of New York looking for a job, I was penniless and hungry. It does you good to quit kidding yourself."

He was right in general, of course, but wrong about one thing. Failure doesn't make you do anything. Walter had the fortitude and the wisdom to use failure. Someone else might have quit long before getting to the stage that night, and been driven off it for good by the experience he had. Without strength, failure can end your dreams. With it, failure can help you make them real.

Michael Massengale and I have mentioned this to each other once or twice, perhaps, in walks we take on the beach in Los Angeles. It's not the kind of thing you dwell on. But you seek that strength in yourself if you're an actor, and you appreciate it in others when their fortitude helps you find your own.

If Walter Huston had quit the theater that night, or on one of those nights singing to a thin crowd on the vaudeville circuit in the Canadian provinces, my life, if I were here at all, might be very different. I think he knew failure very well before he performed Othello that night, and that he'd learned from it. He didn't fear it any longer. He let it be his teacher. He knew its face, and he knew they'd meet again. Michael knows it. I do too. And we're glad.

My father stayed up late that night too, and having read the reviews, he rushed to Walter's room at the Waldorf, hoping I suppose to brace my grandfather for the bad news. When he got to the hallway outside Walter's door, he heard Walter laughing. Walter had already read the papers. He was angry and a little bitter, surprised and disappointed, *but he knew he'd be back for more. He was meeting failure again, and he was laughing with it as he might laugh with an old, tough, trusted teacher. Perhaps the two of them were laughing together.*

Anjelica Huston is an Academy Award–winning actress and critically acclaimed director.

JOE MASSENGALE leafs through the scrapbooks with family photos and clippings from racing successes and his sons' achievements. "Somebody growing up in Marshall, Texas, in those years had to listen to things said to him that no man ought to hear, and certainly no kid," he says. "All those little hateful messages. All those moments when people wanted you to believe you were something less, and that you couldn't have the dreams a person ought to have. That would make a bad impression on anyone. It made some people just give up. I watched it happen.

"My father never did. Maybe it was something he got from his family . . . I don't know. But while he lived there in Marshall and stayed to raise his family, the spirit in him never got down because of being there. He believed in himself and in us, and his heart was stronger than the time and the place. He worked and worked, and it wasn't just to keep us fed. It was to make us see that a better life was possible. That's why he made sure we all went to school and to church, why he set the example he did for us. He never let himself get discouraged. When the money wasn't there or when something bad would happen, well . . . I think he just set himself to working even harder."

Joe was just eleven when responsibility for feeding the family fell to him.

"My older brothers had moved to California to find work in the shipyards, and I was the oldest one at home. My dad was contracting as a log cutter. That's what he really knew to do. He wasn't ever a good farmer. He said, 'Joe, I'll tell you, we need a little money to fix this house and lease some land to farm. I'm going to work at the sawmill in Carthage'—that was about fifteen miles away—'and I'll bring home some money every weekend. You're running this place. You know how to plow, you know how to grow corn and cotton. You've been around, and you should know what you're doing by now. Let's keep that name going—you're a Massengale. Show your daddy what you can do.'

"He'd come home Saturdays and give me fifty cents or so—you could buy ten ice cream cones for that. That was money! And a peanut patty the size of a plate cost a nickel. You could nibble on one of those all week. But it wasn't easy. And it bothered me that I couldn't give him anything, not what I thought I should have given him. But I knew I could do what he asked me. I was ready for that. Those thirty acres had to be plowed, fertilized and planted. My day started before sunup in summertime. Mom would send the girls out with food for lunch and we'd work till nightfall.

"That gave me my work ethic. I liked seeing the results of what I did, and I liked knowing I was providing for my family. Look what it did for me. When I went to high school I was working shining shoes, working at the bus station café, making money. Other guys may have been having fun. I didn't have time to think about it; I was the oldest boy at home and I had to bring something back to them. I was happy when I could go to Solomon's Market around the corner from where I was shining shoes and buy some food to take to my family. That made me feel good, and it kept me going."

Joe pauses again as he remembers Hugh. "I can remember so many times, people looking to my father for his strength. Everyone admired him. They wanted to know what he thought about things. They wanted his leadership. He wasn't but one man like anyone else, but he had that character, and people recognized it in the meetings we'd have in church or at the old Community Center . . . they saw it in the way he took care of his family and in how he worked honestly all the time. He never took a dime he hadn't earned. He took care of other men too, when they worked for him. He made them better at what they did because he held himself up to such a standard. Didn't matter if it was just sawing logs . . . he acted as though it mattered to do it *right*.

"You see things like we all saw, the things we had to live with, and you might think you don't have it in you to get what you want. You might be afraid to try. But in the back of my mind all the time was the idea I could do a little better. I don't know if there was one thing that made me feel that way. My parents never really had the time to sit us down and talk about it with us, not when a kid like me was working ten hours for twenty-five cents. People didn't talk about big dreams and all that. But we saw it in their character, in what my parents did, how they conducted themselves, and that was the example we had. They gave me a way of thinking, I guess."

The study of Joe's home in Los Angeles is full of pictures of moments of victory: Joe's family standing in the winner's circle at Santa Anita and Hollywood Park, photos of his Thoroughbreds winning and pictures of the grandkids.

Joe smiles now, recalling the story a classmate from Pemberton told him during his trip back about the time some students were laughing at him for having too little.

"I was one of the kids from outside of town. There were a few of us who took the log trucks ten or fifteen miles to go to school. The town kids knew who we were. They'd say things. People used to make fun of us for being poor or hungry. You can't laugh at people for what they don't have. You could be down and out sometime yourself, you never know. Made me angry to get put down for what I didn't have, and that's not a bad thing, but being angry gets close to being bitter. You have to be careful. Anger can strengthen you if you use it wisely; bitterness just drags you down. I was angry. It didn't make me vengeful or spiteful or afraid; it didn't make me complain about what I could or couldn't do. It just made me strong.

"I wasn't going to let them tell me what I could be. That's the message some people try to give you—you'd better be happy with what you have, because that's the best you can do. You could get that just living your life where I grew up; being called names by the people, being laughed at by folks who had more than you did. That could bring you down. But I said no, I'm going to do more than this. You need to be strong enough to keep going, and not let yourself get down no matter what anyone else thinks about you. You have to give yourself that chance.

"When I was starting in the landscaping business here in Los Angeles, I knocked on doors. An African-American man looking for work in Beverly Hills in the 1950s and 1960s, I'll tell you, that got some attention. I remember the first day my partner and I went out. We had a rented truck and no place to sleep, no money, and we went to a nice neighborhood and started knocking on doors. The time was going by and we owed that money, so we kept going. A hundred fifty people said no. The hundred-fifty-first said yes."

It takes a lot of strength to keep going like that.

"You bet it does," he says. "But it's a dangerous thing to just sit and want. That's how you get bitter. If you want something, get up and do something, get up and talk to someone. Knock on a door. Just keep moving—you might find what you need."

JOE CAME to Los Angeles permanently in 1947. His eldest brother and his sister-in-law lived in a tiny duplex in South Central Los Angeles, still the heart of the Black community in the city, and they took Joe in while he attended classes at Los Angeles City College and got started in the landscaping business.

South Central was the destination for thousands of people like Joe, all moving west in search of opportunity in a booming postwar economy. He lived just a few blocks from Central Avenue, the long spine of the African-American community that extends south from downtown Los Angeles. The avenue was one of the most influential centers in the country for African-American culture, education, entertainment and activism. Its nickname was "The Brown Broadway." Jazz musician and historian Ted Gioia called the area "an elongated Harlem set down by the Pacific."

The neighborhood grew rapidly during the first half of the twentieth century, due both to the constant influx of new people and to housing practices that were openly racist—people simply declined outright to rent or sell to Blacks—or covertly so, under the "restrictive covenants," the segregationist policies and legal guidelines in zoning and real estate regulations that kept Blacks from living or purchasing property in other areas of Los Angeles, which was sprawling with new developments to the north and west. Bottled in South Central, L.A.'s African-Americans created a city within a city along Central Avenue, opening their own stores, banks, funeral homes and restaurants.

The street was a pageant of Black and White celebrities, limousines and luxury cars, after-hours and breakfast clubs and dance halls holding swing-shift dances at two in the morning for the round-the-clock defense industry workers. John Dolphin's record store literally never closed (the owner gathered the press to witness as he threw away the key). Jelly Roll Morton was a fixture. Louis Armstrong, Lionel Hampton, Nat King Cole and Charlie Mingus all frequented the hot spots. Two-day jam sessions filled Jack's Basket, Brothers, Backstage, the Ritz, Glenn's Backroom and the Casa Blanca, as the musicians all sat in on each other's gigs.

Blacks were unwelcome in the rest of the city, but South Central was a popular destination for many Whites. William Randolph Hearst, Mae West, John Steinbeck and Orson Welles were regulars. Almost inevitably, Central Avenue was a center for the first stirrings of the civil rights movement, as Black musicians denied membership in the White local of the American Federation of Musicians formed their own local, and the Black-owned papers editorialized against the color barrier in films and music.

From the woods outside Marshall, Joe Massengale, Sr., had moved into one of the social centers of Los Angeles, the heart of the West Coast jazz scene. Still in his teens, Joe was dazzled from the moment he stepped out of Union Station. He knew when he heard music in the streets of South Central that Los Angeles was where he wanted to spend the rest of his life.

▦

THE STREETCARS are gone today from Central Avenue, and the traffic is slow as Joe drives his silver pickup south along the avenue for his first visit in years. The old restaurants and chicken joints have given way to franchises and empty lots. All of the old nightclubs have long since disappeared. The Lincoln, the only venue big enough for Duke Ellington's orchestra, is now a church. Babe's and Ricky's, the last survivor of the era, held a farewell performance in 1996 and then closed its doors. An elegant awning with the words CLUB ALABAM faces Central Avenue as a kind of memorial to the legendary nightclub. The Alabam was torn down decades ago. The awning leads only to a fence.

Joe points out all the old locale's nightspots, then heads north toward L.A.'s garment district and the downtown skyscrapers. He says, "Before we head home I want to show you something."

The eastern section of downtown Los Angeles, known here as Skid Row, is a full fifty blocks, the biggest neighborhood of its kind in the United States. The population is impossible to number exactly, but guesses run as high as thirty thousand. People live in homeless missions, in cardboard boxes, in once-splendid hotels such as the Rosslyn or the Cecil, in cars, in tents, under overpasses or just out on the sidewalk. Whole families line up for food from church missions that serve thousands of meals a month. The ordinance against sleeping in public is posted here and there, but with thousands of law-breakers every night, the police are helpless to stop them.

Downtown Los Angeles is coming back to life. The new Staples Center is home to the Lakers, and the new Cathedral of Our Lady of the Angels and the Walt Disney Concert Hall, famous for its Frank Gehry stainless-steel shell, anchor hundreds of millions of dollars in recent investment. But as Joe drives through, the most intractable homeless district in the nation is a netherworld of trash, smoke and despair.

"I used to get clothes in this neighborhood," Joe says. "You could get a custom all-wool suit made for thirty-five dollars. When I was starting out in the tree business and didn't have much, there were mornings when I'd have to bring a suit back down here and pawn it to get money for breakfast. I'd get a few dollars on it, go out and hustle up some work and come back for it at the end of the day.

"I brought my sons down here from time to time when they were boys to show them how it can get for people. Lots of people down here living like this, it's not their fault. Something happens; an illness, some bad luck in business, bad life at home, anything at all; and you never get back out. Some other people, it's the concept they have of life. There's a way of thinking that makes you vulnerable if you aren't careful. Look who it happens to. Millionaires. Movie stars. You can be lucky your whole life, and it'll still catch up with you. If you assume you're invulnerable, it's only going to be worse when it happens. So many of the people I used to love in the music business made it big and lost it all; so many of them made such beauty in their music and such a mess in their lives. Fortitude doesn't mean thinking you can't be hurt. It means being ready, taking what comes when it happens and being strong enough to recover. I used to tell my sons, You can knock me down, but you can't keep me there. That was Papa's attitude too, and he showed us that by example. You can't protect anyone from losses and setbacks, but you can give them the strength to not be defeated."

He looks down an alley. In the shadows a row of makeshift tents is pitched beside an empty warehouse.

"Man," Joe says, "if you don't feel for people like that, there's something wrong with you."

What made the difference for him? "I'd been taught to do better. My parents showed me that. I had a plan. I wouldn't allow myself to think that way, to make the wrong assumptions or to get into trouble. I was a high school graduate; I had brothers here; and I had a better way of thinking, not to be bitter or mean, not to get into trouble. A lot of people just look for fights in life. When I came here, I was just glad to be away from Texas and have a chance to make something of myself. I just wanted a chance to show people the real Joe Massengale and, man, I got my chance. That was in my mind. That kept me straight.

"I bought my first house back there in South Central for six thousand dollars. I was working at North American Aviation during the day, and I'd come home in the afternoon, get in the truck and go out by myself and hustle a tree to work on. It stays light here in the summer until eight or nine at night, and I'd go down halfway to San Diego some nights, doing that. I could save my whole paycheck that way. I always had steady customers. But you can't assume anything. If I didn't go looking for the job, it wouldn't come to me. You need the willing instinct to keep going.

"I grew up around people who believed in themselves, people who were motivated. I got it from them. I had their respect. I knew they loved me and I didn't want to let them down. When you're supposed to be something, if you have any character about yourself, you want to satisfy people too. Not just yourself. You don't want to be any kind of disappointment to anyone. You'd ruin their belief in you, and that hurts them. You owe them your best, just as you owe that to yourself.

"When my sons were with me on the job, I talked a lot with them about that. I'd tell them, If you don't want to climb these trees all your life, you better get yourself an education and prepare yourself for the life you want to live. You know you can do it. If you're strong, you can do anything you put your mind to."

BACK IN Baldwin Hills, downtown looks like a mirage on the horizon as Joe fixes dinner. The homes here are carefully tended, like his. He has jazz on the stereo, and the table is covered with a hot meal. Joe says the same blessing Hugh Massengale said no matter how small supper was back in

Crossroads: "Our Heavenly Father, we are thankful for the food we are about to receive for the nourishment of our bodies, in Jesus' name. Amen."

Before he starts, he nods toward the kitchen counter at a pickle jar half-full of change.

"When I was in my sixties, I had everything a man could ever want. A ten-acre ranch. A stable of Thoroughbreds. Driving a Rolls. That's when I started saving my pocket change. Every day I put a few coins in a jar, just in case. Good thing, because suddenly I was broke. I had to sell the ranch. I had to give most of the horses away. It happens. Doesn't matter who you are. Look at the people in the business that got hit by recession or downturns. Today a big home might make you feel safe. Tomorrow if the economy drops out from under you and you aren't ready, it might be the most dangerous thing in your whole life. You'd better be prepared one way or the other, with flexibility in yourself and an open mind about what you need to do. So when it happened to me, I'd get ten dollars in quarters from the jar to get a hamburger and enough gas to get to Los Angeles, where I had clients and friends. And I'd get here, get a job and go to work.

"All you know is where you've been. You don't know what's going to happen tomorrow. You'd better have something in you in reserve, because the day will come when you need to reach in and find it. That might be all you have to live on until you get back on your feet."

Joe refills the glasses with iced tea.

"When I go to Marshall today, it's hard on me. I had nothing when I was there, no shoes, hungry all the time. Today I have so much. People tell you don't look back, but you have to look back. I know people are trying to be strong telling me to put the past behind me—but I don't want to forget where I came from. It makes me strong thinking about the things my dad had to do to keep us alive and give us hope, and the things I had to do to get where I am. I don't dwell on it, but it's who I am. People struggle. Everybody does. You can resent it or look at it as a source of strength. I was motivated to be something more. I let it make me strong."

That's his gift to me—after all those years of working with my dad and my brothers, I know that I can rely on myself to make my life into what I want it to be, or build myself a career I love. That's how I was raised. Be versatile. Believe in yourself. And give your best in everything you do.

MICHAEL MASSENGALE, Joe's second son, lives in the Mar Vista area of Los Angeles, a neighborhood green with tended lawns and broad-leaved banana palms. Tall and amiable, Michael leaves the front door of his home open for the breeze from the ocean and for his buddy Zane, a neighbor's blond, blue-eyed five-year-old, who wanders in and out of Michael's place as though he lives there. In the living room Michael keeps a set of huge rubber Incredible Hulk hands, bright green and complete with battery-operated sound effects, because Zane likes to come over wearing his own set and duke it out with Michael. Zane recently dragged a babysitter to Michael's door and then abandoned her with Michael's wife, Leticia, while he went off looking for his pal. The baffled babysitter asked, Is Michael another little boy? "Sort of," said Leticia. "But he's fifty years old."

Michael himself is typically barefoot in shorts and a

"Massengale Family Reunion" T-shirt with pictures of his grandparents on the front. Michael's airy house was overrun with bougainvillea and termites when he bought it. He ripped up old carpets and laid down new terra-cotta tiles, knocked out walls, added a bathroom, put in two wood stoves and replaced the window in the back with French doors to make it his own. The walls are hung with abstracts he painted. It's not the biggest house on the block, but he's hosted parties that he catered himself for two hundred people. "Cooking is another creative outlet," he says with a smile. "I steal recipes from all over." He also coaches actors here, and holds business meetings for his real estate practice. Out back are a weight bench and a stack of firewood. He cuts it himself.

On top of the computer in the bedroom is a stack of headshots. On the back of Michael's photo is a long list of coaches and training for dance, acting, vocals, interviewing for the camera, cold reading and improvisational skills, and his acting credits listed in fine print. Michael started acting as a child, left it to follow his older brother Joe Jr. into law school, then returned to it at age forty. One of his skeptical relatives politely reminded him that he was "a little old to be Denzel." Michael laughed and said, "There's already a Denzel, and you know what? I'm going to get even older. And I got a little news for you, I'm doing what I want to do. And I'm loving it."

Was there a single lesson he learned from Joe Sr. that has helped him build the life he has? Michael thought for just a moment and said, "Fortitude."

"Most of my life my father has never had a steady paycheck, something he could count on to be there week in and week out. He's almost always worked for himself. When I think about it, all my brothers, every one of us, we're the same. We've been in the corporate world at times, but we're all independent now. We all chose to go with self-employment and build something ourselves. It's not easy. Some days you're doing nothing and others you're going flat out, but you have the satisfaction of knowing you made your own way.

"I was in the business world for about ten years working as a litigator in the insurance industry. It had its good aspects, but it was the kind of job where they wanted to keep you more or less fixed in a position. You get slotted in where you're productive and it's easy to stay there if that's all you want.

"I got a wake-up call in 1996. I was in a car that spun off an icy road near Lake Tahoe. Cracked two vertebrae in my neck. When they were taking me off on the stretcher, I was flexing my hands and legs just to see if I could move. While I recuperated I realized my life could have been over just like that, or I could have been paralyzed. And I told myself, *From here on, you need to do it differently*.

"I'd done some acting as a child and still had pictures and headshots circulating around, but it had been years since I'd pursued it. I got a call from a producer who wanted me to do his play: here I am, forty, changing careers, coming off nearly getting killed in a serious wreck, and I'm climbing the steps of this musty, creaky old hole-in-the-wall theater on Santa Monica Boulevard to start a new life. I walked into that place and I just said to myself, *Man, welcome home*."

Most of the actors in Los Angeles don't get paid to act. The Screen Actors Guild bluntly describes the practical challenges of making a living as an actor, and advises anyone seeking to join the profession to think of it as part of an overall plan that puts realistic considerations (eating, health coverage, rent, keeping gas in the car) first. Even talented hopefuls must treat it as a luxury they might be unable to pay for during some weeks or months. Plenty of gifted people simply can't afford to do it. You need a plan B to execute your plan A.

"Making a living as an actor tests everything I learned from my dad . . . fortitude, faith, patience," Michael says. "Those are even more important than technical skills or good looks. Good looks are common in acting. You'll be tested on other things. My dad had fortitude that I thought I'd never measure up to, and as I turn fifty, well, maybe I have more of it than I realized. That's what makes the real difference.

"I remember so many times working with him, sitting in the tree truck when it was just pouring outside, a real storm. I'd say, 'Dad, let's go home and get out of this,' and he'd say, 'No, let's wait it out.' It's a business decision, right? Rain or not, if you don't try, you won't get the business. I've thought I'd never have that kind of strength, to just keep trying like he did, knocking on door after door. I used to pray for an iota of it. I didn't think, one, that it would be necessary, and two, that it was in my makeup, but it happened—the older I get, the more I see that the apple doesn't fall far from the tree. I see it in my brothers, too.

"I do mostly theater and television commercials," he says. Michael has done spots for clothing chains, health care organizations—ads with good production values and national audiences. This morning he was up at five to do one for America Online.

"It's a very competitive business. I try to bring some professionalism to it," he says. "It's not playtime for me, any more than working in landscaping was. In both cases you get to love the work of it—the challenge, the effort you need to make, the concentration. It becomes a pleasure. It doesn't matter what the job is, doesn't matter if it's Broadway or some little film you do for nothing. You don't get wrapped up in the ego nonsense when it's about the work. Some people, especially young actors I meet, treat it lightly. Here you are with your own trailer, great food, people helping you all over the place, people watching every move you make, and your ego starts running away with you. Big mistake. None of that is the point.

"And it isn't all fun. There were jobs I wanted to quit. I just did a film with four straight weekends of night shoots, call times at midnight. It was a strain. But nothing comes to a quitter. You don't bail on things when something else comes along. Paid or not, hard or not, you have to learn about fortitude and commitment. You take the good ones when you can and you see it through. That's the real fun of it. Doing it right, nailing the line, giving your best.

"My dad used to say, 'You might knock me down but I'll get up.' And he's right—you will get knocked down. I might go on a hundred auditions a year to get three jobs. When I land one, it's a coup.

"This morning I was out of here before sunup to drive to this commercial. Some actors don't do commercials. I understand that if you're a certain type of actor and it might compromise a show or something you're on, but just to say I don't do commercials because I did *Macbeth* off-Broadway, well . . . that's unrealistic. *Pride goeth before destruction*, right? I just say, thank God, here I am doing what makes me happy."

One of the cell phones on the table buzzes. Michael interrupts to take the call and returns in a few minutes. "Speaking of fortitude," he says. "That's a deal I'm going to have to nurse for a while. It's an escrow on two pieces of land in the Pacific Palisades. I'm both the listing agent and I represent the buyers. When you do what's known as a dual agency, you have to be careful to treat everyone with flawless integrity and make sure everyone is happy. This is a big sale and it'll take time. Doesn't happen by magic. I'll need to be with it every step of the way.

"My dad always approached work like that. Didn't matter what he was doing, the tree business or in racing or being a disk jockey or speaking in church. He got up at five A.M. looking forward to the day. Man, that's fortitude. He'd tell us, I'm up, so everybody else get up, and we all did. I remember once when I'd come home from college and we were watching the *Today* show. My dad said to us, 'Hey, those guys already got their money. Let's go get *ours*.' His motivation was to succeed every day, *every day*. We worked Saturdays and Sundays, no big deal; emergency work, working in storms and wind and rain, working in the middle of the night. That was the job.

"You run into every kind of person in the tree business. Imagine the reactions we got during the 1960s, 1970s, a truckload of young African-American men knocking on doors in Palm Springs and Beverly Hills—we'd meet anyone and everyone—we'd work for the very wealthy but we could be run off by the gardener if he felt we're in his space, or the neighbor would offer advice over the back fence suggesting that we were making too much money. The best acting lessons I ever got came from working in Beverly Hills and Burbank and San Diego. Some days I'd be up a hundred feet in a eucalyptus with a chain saw in my hand and I'll tell you, there's a lot of ways to get hurt doing that if you aren't paying attention. Dad would be on the ground telling me what to do, where to step, how to do the job right. He was the first and best director I ever had. He paid attention to every stage of the job, appearances, courtesies, the way we conducted ourselves. We had clean uniforms. The truck was washed. My dad made sure that when we rang the doorbell on a house, we stepped back a few feet so people coming to the door could get a clear look at us. The quality of the work itself was a given. We were good at what we did. But that was only part of it, and in many ways the easiest part. Getting paid, making sure the client was happy, leaving a good impression, those were all just as important.

"Believe me, physical labor is mostly about thinking, about paying attention where it matters. That's why it's fun, and why it's such great training for an actor. It doesn't matter if it's athletics or acting or selling. Every kind of work has a physical component to it, whether you're wearing a suit in a courtroom or a coverall in a tree. You have to have your mind and your body together, working in sync, because everything about you is part of the impression you make, even on yourself. How you feel in the situation is half the job. Are you comfortable, are you focused, are you conveying in every way that you're professional, that you can be trusted, that you're confident in who you are? And can you handle it when it gets rough without losing your composure?

"One of the biggest jobs we ever had was removing a grove of big trees from a property in West Los Angeles. Well, my dad told the owner, 'Sure, we can do that'—and we'd never taken on anything that big. These were enormous trees! And we had ten days to do it. I spent a lot of time seventy, eighty feet up, roped to a limb with a safety belt, taking direction from my dad with that chain saw in my hand. It's hard and it's hazardous—you want to learn how to take direction as an actor? That's one good lesson right there. The man spotting on the ground tells you where to step, and you better believe you don't argue.

"At the end of the ten days we had the job done and the client was taking us all to breakfast. That felt great. Jobs like that gave me a lot of faith in myself, in my own fortitude, to be able to work that way, and that carries over into what I do now.

"I still like to work like that—if my dad called me with a tree job tomorrow, I'd be glad to do it.

"That's his gift to me—after all those years of working with my dad and my brothers, I know that I can rely on myself to make this house into what I want it to be, or build myself a career I love, and be a good husband to my wife. That's how I was raised. Be versatile. Believe in yourself and your strength. And give your best to everything you do."

Someone coming from Joe's circumstances might have felt he had too much to overcome. Michael agrees, but then, not everyone is his father.

"You could say Joe Massengale had a right to fail, a right to lose, coming from nothing as he did. But he wanted more and he decided he had the strength to make it a reality. He'd see people doing well and ask, Why can't I have that? He went to work, saved his money and built a life for himself. He could have listened to other people tell him his limitations but he didn't. He never settled for less than the best from himself. Failure was okay. Losing wasn't. That's his fortitude, and that's what he gave me. I'll keep going. Let them say no. I'll keep going. I'll fall on my face but that's not the same as losing—you lose when you don't make the attempt.

"At age sixty my dad went broke. He'd gone through a divorce, the economy went south, he had some serious debt and he just couldn't get it going. Sold his ranch and put all his stuff in storage and he moved in with me for a year. At age sixty he started all over. He went out every day. He never faltered. In a year he'd amassed a small fortune just going to work every day in the tree business. He never felt defeated.

"You got to wake up pretty early in the morning to tell us what we can and can't do. My dad's a guy who's done everything but die, seen everything but God and been everywhere but heaven. And he's still here. And so am I. I wake up every day and say, Another golden opportunity to do something. I might fall on my face today but I'm up. That was Joe: I'm up, everybody get up. You won't get anything laying around here."

ON A wet winter evening, Michael's work takes him to the auditorium at Manchester High School south of downtown Los Angeles to rehearse a labor of love.

North on South Central Avenue is a musical about the golden age of jazz in Los Angeles, the one Michael's father saw first-hand half a century ago. The chilly auditorium is the best space available tonight to squeeze in two practice sessions before a benefit performance in a few days.

The play needs a home. It was held over through extended runs at the Stella Adler Theatre in Hollywood, at the Barnsdall Gallery Theatre and the Madrid Theatre in Canoga Park and it was selected as "grand opening performance" for the Miles Memorial Playhouse in Santa Monica. *The Los Angeles Times* compared it to the Oscar-winning *Chicago*. But it still has no regular base. Those cast members who can attend tonight come after their paying jobs through rush-hour traffic from all over the city. There is no set to work with, no props, only a piano and a set of congas to fill in for a six-piece band, and you can see your breath indoors, but after five years together, the actors and musicians know the play so well that this run-through is more of a reunion than a rehearsal. No one needs a script.

The dancers warm up in the back of the huge hall as the actors get settled. It's cold enough for people to wear scarves and gloves while they work. The director calls for "energy, energy, energy!" as Michael, sitting downstage on a folding chair, ages himself thirty years to become an elderly Central Avenue resident. After years of working on it, Michael slips into the role in moments.

Most of *North on South Central Avenue* takes place in flashbacks. The scene moves back and forth between the bus stop today and the Avenue in its heyday to capture the glamour and the music of the era "when swing was the thing, when jazz was king," told unvarnished, nostalgic but not naive, with the euphoria of some of the best music ever made in the United States and the pain of watching it all disappear as South Central declined.

The director gives the cast additional tips about projecting, but this is really just a tune-up. When they break up that night, they know they're ready.

Show night, a week later, is Super Bowl Sunday, probably the single worst night of the year to hold a one-night-only performance, but the house is full at the Henry Fonda Music Box in Hollywood. A jewel from the grand old days of L.A. nightlife, it couldn't be better suited for staging *North on South Central Avenue*. The interior is lush with deep blue and crimson and gilt. The area before the stage is set up supper-club style, with tables and chairs. The audience is part of the show.

The performance tonight is a benefit for breast cancer research. In the announcements before the show, the directors thank the crowd and acknowledge some special guests, among them Buddy Collette, one of the old soldiers of South Central jazz from Joe Sr.'s day, now well into his eighties. The cast invites the house to a reception with hors d'oeuvres and dessert in the lobby after the show. They don't say that their performances this evening are all donated, that they catered the reception themselves, and had only hours earlier this afternoon for their tech rehearsal to prepare the sound and lighting before the show. But morale is high. The cast has a special announcement to make after the performance.

The red curtain stays down and the piano plays "They Can't Take That Away from Me" as people settle. Joe Massengale, Sr., takes his seat and notes that the mixed crowd looks just like the ones back at the clubs he loved as a teenager: "It used to be like this back at Central Avenue. All kinds of people having fun like this."

The only visible set is a sign, BUS STOP, CENTRAL AVE., and a bench at audience level, off the stage and to the left. As the lights dim, an elderly man in a fedora and gold-rimmed glasses moves slowly through the crowd and takes a seat beside a teenage kid to wait for the 54 southbound bus. With an hour to talk until the next one comes, Willie tells him about the Central that once was, about the Blacks who migrated westward from Louisiana and Mississippi and Texas looking for opportunity and brought their music along.

North on South Central follows young Willie coming from Mississippi to Los Angeles, leaving his beloved wife, Birdlegs, behind until he can find work and send for her. Most of the action takes place inside the Alabam, where Willie lands a job as night security guard in the heart of the legendary music scene.

The story interweaves Willie's tale with that of the Alabam's owners, L. C. and Eloise Lomax, his surrogate family, and their adversaries, the local White mobster Manny Brandenberg and his Black partner Curtis Moseley, who seek to take over the club. As in the real Alabam, many of the best entertainers of the day make appearances: Ella Fitzgerald, Dorothy Dandridge, Sarah Vaughan, Billie Holiday, Little Walter, Nat King Cole and Dinah Washington sing the classics of the day. It's not all fun. The club's dangers, drunks and drugs are there to see. Willie has to be warned off the invitations of the singers while Birdlegs is still waiting to be summoned from Mississippi. Lady Day is barely able to stand through "God Bless the Child," and she pulls a knife on an overzealous fan who wants more than an encore. Willie notes that the White patrons of the club called it "slumming" to visit the neighborhood.

"Fifty years on South Central . . ." says the young man.

"Sounds like it was a happening place back then. Wish it could be like that now."

"It can be," Willie says. "It can. Y'all just need to stop spraying so much paint and bullets round here. Nothin' a good old Mississippi Ass Whippin' won't cure . . . Yep, y'all can turn it around, son. 'Cause, see, there's always more than one way to handle your differences. I'm Willie Robinson, pleased to make your acquaintance . . ."

The ending is Michael's work. The kid asks what became of all the old clubs, and Willie looks wistful as he recites the obituary of Central Avenue, naming the venues long since gone: the Downbeat, Club Memo, Ivy's Chicken Shack, the Plantation, Club Alabam, recounting for the audience the decline Joe watched: "The Central Avenue streetcars were replaced by automobiles. Major industries relocated to the suburbs after the Korean War. Unemployment began to rise and local people couldn't afford to pay for entertainment. So the great clubs slowly began to decline. Your 'rap' scene has now taken the place of the 'jazz' scene, and the delicate memories of time still have yet to reinvent themselves for history's sake."

Most painful to Old Willie is the loss of Birdlegs, killed in a robbery attempt in South Central not long before. This is the moment an actor lives for: after a night of raucous, thumping music, the Music Box is silent. Three hundred people hold their breath as Old Willie sees her phantom, tells her he misses her and promises to join her soon.

A reprise of "This Joint Is Jumpin' " wraps it up to a standing ovation.

After an extended curtain call, Michael Massengale takes the stage and holds up nine fingers to announce that *North on*

South Central Avenue has just received nine nominations for NAACP Theatre Awards, including Best Ensemble, Best Playwright and Best Director. Everyone in the cast wants the biggest prize of all: Broadway.

North on South Central is a special investment for Michael in several ways. As one of the backers of the show, he has a business stake in its success. As an actor it's been a recurring role for him, something he keeps coming back to with new ideas to test. And it's a tribute not only to Joe, but to other people Michael has known and loved going back in his family history to Marshall.

"When I do Old Willie, I'm playing my father, my uncle, my grandmother; real people I saw, people I knew," he says after the show. "My dad used to tell me about Central Avenue all the time. When I first auditioned for it in 1999, I was coming along as an actor. I wasn't very good, but the part meant so much to me that I built myself into it. My character's history parallels that of my dad. Coming in on the Sunset Limited to Union Station there. Living down there in South Central in a house so little you had to walk outside to turn around. He just loved that neighborhood, especially coming from East Texas, being what, eighteen, nineteen, new to the city and seeing how things could be for people who were used to having next to nothing. He used to tell us all the time about Ivy's Chicken Shack and the Alabam. He just fell in love with Los Angeles then and there.

"My father is the basis for Old Willie. His plain-spoken easy way with people, that rapport he has. He didn't put on an air—he just talked like who he was. People would ask us why my brothers and I didn't take over his tree business. It was because we didn't have what he had in that way. It wasn't really so much the way he did the work, because we did the actual work in the same way. But that manner, that personal quality, that was his. I'd tell people, I'll take a fraction of it if it's genetic, but I couldn't do that like he did it. Imagine being that flexible, dealing like he did with all those different people over the years. People recognized that genuineness in him. I guess where I do the same thing is as an actor now. His stage was somebody's front yard. Mine is the one in the theater.

"My dad showed me something I never forgot: the difference between faking and acting. People can spot it. You can deliver a great technical performance with the accent and the walk and the mental makeup you put on and it can still lack a heartbeat. Real acting has life to it—people forget you're acting and they take your character as a real living thing. That's what I try to do, get deeper and deeper. My intent is to reach that audience, not just impress them with technique. I want to touch them, take them on a trip, make them feel, make them laugh and cry. Give them the real experience of all those moments. I'm still learning."

Michael smiles at the memory of his work back when he resumed acting after so many years away. "I remember getting singled out in a bad review, man . . . it mentioned me as a failure *by name*. I wanted to go out and buy every copy of the paper and bury what that critic had said about me. But that guy was right. I had a bad night, opening-night anxiety, inexperience, and I just didn't get it together. But I came back. I was bad until I got good. I learned. Now I'm working all the time because I stuck with it. My dad said it to me again and again when I was a kid: you can knock me down, but I'll keep getting back up. That was the best acting training I could have asked for. I'll use every skill I have, and if I don't have the skills, I'll work to get them. That's my strength as an actor. It's not my gifts. I'm not the most talented actor I know. But when I fail, I pay attention, and listen for a better idea, and next time I'm better.

"I've seen an interview with Anthony Hopkins about that same idea. Here's an Oscar-winning actor, brilliant on the stage, on the screen, a man with nothing to prove, and he said that before the first day of rehearsing a play or shooting a movie he'll have read the script two hundred times. Hopkins gets hired on his name alone. He could coast on his reputation. But he's doing the work like it's his first role and he feels lucky to get it. It's not about fame for him. He still does it to *get better*. Anjelica Huston, another example. She got knocked down her first time out. Came back and won the Oscar and a Golden Globe. She's directing. She's never stopped working to grow.

"That's fortitude. I still see actors who think that strength is having a powerful agent or strong opinions. You see people throwing their weight around on a set, being demanding. It's a dangerous way to think of strength, because everybody's replaceable. You might be strong this afternoon, okay, but tomorrow you're out of a job. The actors I look up to show their strength by acting with conviction. They make mistakes all the time, but they do it with decisiveness, taking courageous chances, really putting themselves at risk, being scared if that's what it takes, willing to get a bad review, knowing for certain that they'll be knocked down hard. And they learn from it and they get back up. The courage to be vulnerable means being real, because that's life. We're vulnerable. My dad lived that every day of his life when he was a kid. Bring that truth to a role, and the role comes to life. To me that's fortitude: the strength to start fresh every day, to learn and be open, to listen for every idea that's going to make you better. My dad gave that to me. That's why I love what I do."

North on South Central Avenue took four of the nine 2004 NAACP Theatre Awards for which it was nominated.

Next stop: Broadway.

LESSON THREE

PRIDE

Preface by Rafer Johnson

The best moment in any competition isn't at the finish line, or even on the winner's platform when the contest is over. It's at the beginning, when you don't know what the outcome will be. You feel your nerves tingling and your muscles ready, straining to move. You focus your mind and calm your breathing. All the work you've done to prepare for this moment comes back to you.

You see your competition, who look bigger or stronger or faster than you, and you know you need to draw deep on something that isn't so much of the body as it is of the spirit. You draw on pride.

Some of the greatest competitors I've ever seen on the athletic field and in life were the ones whose pride sustained them when their physical gifts gave out. They drew on that invisible strength. They didn't need to win the race to be proud; they started the race with it. It permitted them nothing less than giving their best. And when the last ten yards seemed longer than the first ninety or the first thousand, their pride was the fuel that drove them on.

Pride isn't about what you deserve or what you'll take. It's more about what you give.

Remember, pride comes with hazards. The Scriptures warn again and again of misplaced pride, the pride that stiffens into arrogance. At best it's foolishness, and at worst it's a deadly sin: "Pride goeth before destruction," says

Proverbs, "and an haughty spirit before a fall." For some people, the danger of pride is that it invites them to stay the same. We might be very proud of a narrow aspect of ourselves, or proud of who we are right now, or of an accomplishment from our past. That kind of pride may be richly deserved, but nevertheless, pride that stands still is complacency. It closes your mind to new ideas, and closes your ears when you need to listen.

When I was competing I hated to lose, and I still do. But I had enough wisdom to be taught by people who knew how to help me reach for my best effort. One of the best compliments I was ever paid was when Ducky Drake, my track coach at UCLA, told me that my greatest asset as an athlete wasn't my talent. It was that I could listen and take instruction. We've all seen vastly gifted people who were too proud to do that. Their talent didn't get tested, didn't get strengthened. Ultimately it may have gone to waste.

Of all the people I've met, some of the ones who deserved the most to be proud were the ones who never thought to wear their pride on their sleeve. They started proud, tested it, used it, invested it—they gave their pride away in the effort to make their own lives and the lives of others better. My mother, brothers and sisters, my wife and children, friends I've admired, fellow athletes . . . different as they were, what they had in common was an unusual kind of pride. They had a curiosity about life, the faith in themselves to ask questions and experience the unfamiliar, and the willingness to listen and learn. They were less proud of what they were than of what they sought to be, and what they were willing to do for it. Don't ever mistake that kind *of quiet, steady faith for weakness. A person with that kind of pride can leave you in the dust on the track. They aren't competing against you. They might be concentrating so intently they barely know you're there. They're testing themselves, looking within for any lapse or weakness, and using their pride to fuel them to get better.*

I know that very few people have had the chance I had to stand on the platform at the Olympics and receive a gold medal, and I am grateful for the moment I had there. But other moments in my life have meant more to me, and taught me more about pride. The most satisfying pride I've ever seen was what lights up the faces of the kids I work with in the Special Olympics. The joy of competition is so pure in them—simply taking part lifts their hearts. Their pride defeats silence with laughter, sadness with delight. They feel like winners, some of them for the first time in their lives. I think it's because they have what pride should give us all, a new vision of themselves, and the feeling that we can win over any obstacle that life puts in our path.

As a father and as a husband, it's that lesson I'd want to pass along to my family. No matter what race you're in, no matter what career, no matter what gets between you and your dreams, start the race with pride in your heart—and run to be the best that you can be.

Rafer Johnson is an Olympic gold medalist and a three-time world record holder in the decathlon. In 1969, he helped to found California Special Olympics to inspire and serve individuals with mental retardation. He still serves the organization today.

WORKING THE early shift at North American Aviation and landscaping in the afternoons made it easy for Joe Massengale to save money. He had been promoted twice at the aircraft company, so the work was steady and the future looked secure. By the mid-1960s, Joe's first marriage was over, but he was still a father with obligations he wanted to keep. Many men might have settled in at a steady career as a mechanic. Instead, Joe rolled the dice on something he had dreamed of since he moved to Los Angeles. With no experience, he approached a radio station and told them he was ready to host his own show.

"I just decided I wanted to do it," Joe says as he climbs into his pickup for a drive around his old music haunts. "I'd come up two grades as a mechanic, but I never really loved the work. You can't spend your whole life doing something you don't love. I loved music. So I called a little thousand-watt station, KFOX in Long Beach, and said, 'My name is Joe Massengale. I do announcements at my church and I'm a good public speaker. I want to go on the radio.' Keep in mind, it was a lot more open then than it is now. There were wildcat DJs and independent record labels popping up all over Los Angeles, so this wasn't as crazy as you might imagine. Many people got famous overnight by just knocking on doors and talking their way into the business. That's how it was; young people hustling. I could do that. I was daring enough to ask. I always needed to challenge myself. I wanted to get my name out there.

"The man at KFOX asked me, 'What experience do you have?' I said, 'Well, I don't have any.' He asked, 'Do you have any sponsors?' I said, 'No, but I can get one.' He thought a moment and said, 'Here's what I'll do. I have a half hour slot on Sunday afternoons, five to five-thirty. Go get a sponsor and I'll give you a chance.'"

It was a minimal risk for the station. KFOX billed itself as "The Country King," aiming its programming at Navy and dock personnel working at the harbor. Sundays were given to religious and public service shows until the station went off the air at midnight. The listening audience on Sunday afternoons would be very small. It was a perfect time to let a novice get some practice.

"Well," Joe says, "I started looking for sponsors. I went to a car dealer here in South Central, talked to the owner and told him what I had in mind: a spiritual program of sacred songs. I needed about sixty dollars a week. He gave me fifty and said if he noticed results from the sales, he'd cover the show. I went home that afternoon and wrote my first radio spot." Joe's voice slips a notch into a smooth Texas baritone: " '*Eric's Motor Sales, Florence and Figueroa in downtown Los Angeles—if you're shopping for a car, be sure and stop in to see them at Eric's Motor Sales at Florence and Figueroa and also downtown at 1945 South Figueroa. Be sure to say that Joe Massengale sent you.*' And he loved it.

"Man, I'll never forget the first time I heard that announcer say. 'It's time for the Joe Massengale Program of Sacred Songs—*and here's Joe!*' And I could hardly say a word!

"I played those beautiful spirituals, Jackson Southernaires, Willie Banks and the Messengers, Dixie Hummingbirds, The Williams Brothers, The Sensational Nightingales, The Soul Stirrers—that was Sam Cooke's gospel group, The Pilgrim Travelers, The Swan Silvertones . . . but oh, I was nervous. I was just running my mouth on about anything to fill the time, and I was very glad when that half hour was over. The engineer gave me a tape of that show to listen to and study. I bought one of those big old reel-to-reel tape recorders to play that tape and I'll tell you, I listened to that awful show a hundred times that week. Brought in some friends to hear it with me, over and over, and they just tore me apart. But I learned. I did a lot better the second time—the announcer said to me afterwards, 'Man, what *happened* to you this week? You're gonna be *good*.'"

For Joe Massengale, spinning spirituals on a country station when no one was listening was just one more version of the coveted thing everyone else was looking for: a way in.

By 1956, Joe had enough experience to find a bigger audience with KALI, a Pasadena station, and this time his show was pure pop. Here he helped break new ground: he was one of the rare DJs in the city who played records by both Black and White artists. Los Angeles was where rhythm and blues, soul, gospel, country, and classic ballads were converging like streams into a river of new sound, and Joe was playing it every night. "I played Elvis Presley and Buddy Holly and Ritchie Valens and Frank Sinatra," he says, "anything I liked. I never cared for the racial angle on music. My taste was always more about what I enjoyed than it was about race. My dad was the same way. He sang all the time, love songs and gospel, just so long as it was pretty. I'm that way too. I loved Sam Cooke and Dick Haynes and The Platters and Sinatra. It was about the music. Race just didn't come in to it."

A typical day would find him out of the house at seven in the morning. "I'd get in this 1936 Ford one-ton, a raggedy old pickup truck I'd bought for a hundred dollars. I'd hustle up some tree work door-to-door in Pasadena and wrap it up before the show at 1:30. I'd stop in a service station with soap and a towel and wash up, then sneak into the studio and close the door. They never knew I was in there in coveralls," he laughs. "Spin a few records, 'Bye Bye Love,' 'That'll Be the Day,' a little Tony Bennett, some Ray Charles, then do some spots. I never was much of a reader," he continues, "but I could talk on my feet better than anyone. I learned that in the tree business, that pleasant comfortable way of talking. It makes people feel at ease. The station never wrote much scripted material for me because I was always more relaxed just going on my own. So some days I'd be out doing remotes in a local supermarket, just going up and down the aisles with a microphone talking with people, mentioning the special items on sale, chatting with the owners. I always liked talking with people, and it came naturally. Then I'd go back to the station and do the 6 to 7 P.M. show. More of that music, Elvis, James Brown. Everything like that. So much was happening, you couldn't keep up with the music."

"The best, though, was the last show I did. In 1959 I got a late-night gig in Long Beach, KGER. That's where things really heated up. Midnight to two, and this was all before the freeways around here were built so I'd have to hustle from Pasadena to Long Beach in that old truck. That's a long haul, I'll tell you. But after a while I could do it from down here in South Central. Right there." He points from the truck to an empty lot beside a liquor store. "Right there, 4367 Western Avenue. It was a studio then, and I spent a lot of the time there. I had a cool style, easy sort of, conversational. Some of the jocks cracked a lot of jokes and some were gospel-style talkers, loud and preachy-sounding. A few of the jocks talked more jive. I never copied anyone, never tried to make it a Black show or a White show. I just did my thing.

"People would stop by the show from all over—Pat Boone, Carol Jarvis—remember 'Rebel' and 'Golden Boy'? That's her. Nice lady. The Platters . . . they'd come in and do interviews with me and we'd spin some records and talk. Man, I was thirty years old and felt like I had this town right in my hand."

Ten-sixty-five East Vernon, not far from the house where Joe first lived when he came to Los Angeles, was the heart of the scene: station KRKD, just 250-watts, broadcasting live round the clock from John Dolphin's legendary record store. Producer, talent manager, second-story man, Dolphin was a guru for the young musicians and producers, Black and White, in the city. Phil Spector and Sonny Bono shopped and learned there. "John Dolphin gave me a ton of records," Joe says, smiling. "I got lots of records there, and I always listened to the shows because I wanted to hear what they were spinning. If you wanted to meet people in the music business, that's where you went."

A personal favorite of Joe's, both for his music and his friendship, was Sam Cooke. "'The fabulous Sam Cooke,' I called him," Joe says. "Just the nicest man, a wonderful man, and oh, what a voice. Great singer, great writer . . . he'd just sit and create right in front of you. He'd write a song while you were watching and say, 'That's a hit!'

"Sam and I were about the same age. He was from Mississippi, not too far really from where I came from, and he was a bridge between gospel and soul and rock—you know he started with The Soul Stirrers, singing gospel? I used to play a lot of those songs on my first program, 'Nearer to Thee' and 'Touch the Hem of His Garment.' When he came on my show he'd made 'You Send Me' with the Keen label and it wasn't going anywhere. Sam was still driving a cab here in town to make ends meet before he finally broke through—can you believe that, Sam Cooke hustling as a cabbie? Then he just caught fire. 'Wonderful World,' *The Ed Sullivan Show*. Most beautiful tenor I ever heard, and pretty soon the whole country thought so too.

"The last time I saw him must have been just a few weeks before he was killed. I'd been playing his records all night, 'Sad Mood,' 'Bring It On Home to Me,' 'Another Saturday Night,' 'Twisting the Night Away,' and I got a call from Zola Taylor to come to a party after the show. Sam was there, tending bar and just having fun. He said, 'Joe, man, thanks so much, you made me a star again tonight.' We stayed up talking and laughing. He was what, twenty-nine, thirty years old.

There was no telling what he was capable of doing. By then he'd already crossed over from the segregated clubs—he was playing Vegas in front of all kinds of people and everyone loved him. He was creating his own story. That was the last time I saw him. Just a few weeks later he was gone." Cooke died in a shooting in South Central in December 1964. All of Los Angeles mourned, and two hundred thousand people crowded a three-day farewell where Lou Rawls and Ray Charles sang. "I knew so many talented young people who didn't make it. Sam, Jesse Belvin, Frankie Lymon . . . it's heartbreaking to see those gifts get lost. There was a lesson there in their lives for me about pride, and what it can cost you."

Joe tried his own hand at producing and even singing in 1962 with a tune he penned in his driveway, "Only One Girl." Backing him was a group he managed briefly, The Rivingtons, who made R&B hits of "Papa Oom-Mow-Mow" and "The Bird's the Word." Instead of trying to crack the jammed Los Angeles market, Joe promoted it along with "Papa Oom-Mow-Mow" in the more accessible markets in Dallas and Houston, closing a circle that had started in 1946 when he first saw The Ink Spots play at the Houston Auditorium and got the bug to go to Los Angeles. Before long he had a "Pick of the Week" in East Texas, and he and his band came home to tour the radio stations and savor the applause. They met Sam Cooke and B.B. King in Houston along with the R&B great Floyd Dixon, an old friend from Marshall. Things almost got out of hand in a small town outside Dallas.

"When my dad was a young man he hoboed from Dallas down to Carthage. You know how it was. A freight train's going by, you jump in, and when it got to where you wanted to go, it slows down and you jump out. My dad was on the train and he fell asleep in a boxcar. They switched the cars out in a little town close to Dallas. One of the most racist places you ever saw, and that's where he woke up. *Not* a place where you wanted to find yourself if you were a Black man early in the twentieth century. They had a sign up—a *sign*—that showed a Black man with a bindle on his back and the sun setting overhead, and it read, 'Nigger, don't let the sun go down on you in this city.' He said to himself, 'Oh my Lord, I better find a way to get out of here fast.' Some White boys were playing around the boxcars in the railyard. Kids, twelve, fourteen years old. One of them looked in the car and saw my dad. He yelled out, 'There's a nigger in there!' Papa jumped out and started running down the tracks, with them right behind. He outran two of them, but the third one picked up a railroad spike and hit my dad in the small of the back. Knocked him down. He got up hurt and kept on running. His back was never right after that. I don't know how he got home to Marshall alive.

"So we're down there in 1962 touring the radio stations in East Texas and 'Only One Girl' comes on in the car. So we stopped the car in that same town with the radio on loud, too loud, and called home on a pay phone so people back home could hear the music with us. Well, one of the local police officers stopped . . . a White cop and a car full of Black men making a disturbance in that place . . . I'll tell you, I was just thinking of my dad. The cop was actually nice about it—he understood, even shook my hand, and I gave him some records for his daughter. We all signed them and everything.

We didn't stay around long, though, I'll say that. That's a chance you don't take. We were proud, no doubt about it, but we weren't stupid."

Los Angeles promoters and producers gave records by the hundred to every DJ in town. Joe's garage stacked up with them so quickly he and his brother opened a shop, Bop City Records, at Jefferson and Western, and it too became a magnet for performers. It's a KFC today, but in its day, he remembers, "We'd have limos outside with performers stopping by all hours. James Brown came in one night . . . he'd heard the show and I'd play his records all the time. Man, what a talent. How many times has he been at the top of the charts? Fifteen, sixteen at least. We sat up late that night talking, just him and me. He said, 'Joe, you know one thing? I've had it all and I've lost it all. If I ever make any money again I'll be careful this time, I really will.'

"So many of those performers were like that, you know? Kids from the South, no education, no maturity, just raw talent, and they make a million fast and think those good times are going to last forever. Big cars, big houses, and soon they're right back where they started and wondering why, or worse. Happens to anyone; nobody is safe from it. So many of the rock and roll kids died in Hollywood in those years, talented kids, people I met, people whose music I played. Drugs or liquor or guns . . . driving too fast or living too fast and you forget just for a second. One moment of that kind of pride. That's all it takes.

"I was still working trimming trees even then—business was better than ever, in fact, and that was my living. Didn't matter what I was doing the night before. If I was up talking with someone who was at the top of the charts, next morning I was up early and knocking on doors."

In 1964 Joe met Zola Taylor at the racetrack, and the attraction was fast and mutual. The petite lead singer of The Platters was in her early twenties and a global hit. "Zola was just a tiny thing. They called her Lil' Bit. Red hair, big smile. Beautiful voice. We went out that night and had a great time. I went for her 100 percent, and she went for me. I started seeing her every day when she was in Los Angeles. I thought we'd be getting married. But her band had had its problems—four of them got arrested in Cincinnati on vice charges, and Zola was living too fast herself. She and Frankie Lymon toured the world together when The Platters and The Teenagers were at the top, and it came out later that they were involved. Remember 'Why Do Fools Fall in Love'? That was Frankie Lymon. Good voice, but when I saw him sing, he was such a mess he could hardly stand up. He'd been a heroin user for years—keep in mind, he was still really just a kid—and it destroyed all that talent. Killed him eventually. Tragic. The Platters ended up replacing Zola, too . . . she'd been all over the world with them, made millions, and she ended up with a few thousand dollars. Lost it all.

"That'll teach you something about pride, won't it? You don't have to see many gifted people lose everything and break their families' hearts to know better. It's just pride, that's all . . . they hear people telling them anything they want to hear, and they get too proud, and it's the same story over and over. Those old spirituals I played back at KFOX were some pretty good training for living as a DJ in those years. If you're blessed with talent, keep in mind what Proverbs tells you: '*A man's pride shall bring him low: but honour shall uphold the humble in spirit.*' I made sure my sons knew that too. Pride needs balance. It's easy to be proud of something—when you think about it, plenty of people are good at something, good-looking, talented or smart or gifted somehow. Talent isn't hard to find, especially here in Los Angeles. Everybody's talented here. But the discipline it takes to make it last, to keep your eye on bigger things, to keep your head—that's what makes the difference, and that's rare. Discipline keeps the pride in its place. Talent might open the doors for you, but discipline will keep you there."

Joe laughs and continues, "One of my tree clients referred me to a friend and told the friend, 'Let me tell you about Joe Massengale. He just believes he's the best in the business and you'll have to listen to him brag about it at least fifteen minutes. But he's the best man for the job. He backs it all up.' Know who that was? Mrs. Bolger, Ray Bolger's wife. I saw him just the other night in *The Wizard of Oz*—he was the Scarecrow, remember? I did tree work for thirty years on a big place they had here. The first time I was out there I worked for three days and Ray liked the work so much he came out and shook my hand and said, 'Joe, you're worth dancing for,' and he cut a little step right there in the driveway. We were friends from that day on.

"You know, the truth is, my work might not be better than anyone else's. I'm not the only one in Los Angeles who does good landscaping. But I talk to people like that because I want them to understand how much I believe in myself and in how much they can believe in me too. It's exactly the same way I went about being on the radio, hustling for jobs and for sponsors, practicing to get better—working at it instead of just be-lieving I was good enough to take things for granted. When I tell my clients I'm the best, just like when I told those radio stations I could be on the air, it's not bragging—it's making a promise to them and to me. I can show them the technical differences if they want to know—some trimmers leave things too heavy, take too much, leave things asymmetrical. But I know my way around a tree and I can make it beautiful. I know my way around a studio and I can entertain an audi-ence. You value your home and your time. Either way, you want the best. I earn my pride by respecting yours.

"Character is what you are; reputation is what folks *think* you are. You have to build both the best you can. Character without the reputation means you lose to someone who just talks a better game than you do; reputation without the char-acter means you don't have the discipline to keep your prom-ises, and you don't have customers for long like that. My work is about both. L.A.'s a place where you can make a good repu-tation easily; just buy an ad or put up a billboard and people will think you know what you're doing. But can you keep the promise? Will your work be that good the second time?

"Pride," he goes on, "isn't thinking you're better than any-one else. It's having the discipline to improve, to see what you're doing wrong, see how you can do it better. It's not handed to you. You create it in yourself. Every failure I had gave me something I could use. That's what I taught my sons, to be proud enough and strong enough to fail if it happened and to keep coming back.

"When I get a job, I need to make sure that every leaf I can see is cleaned up. If I step on a little flower in the garden, small as your little finger, I knock on the client's door and tell them. I've had guys work for me tell me, 'That flower's an inch tall, it's nothing, they'll never notice.' I say, 'It has to be something because somebody put it there. It didn't just grow. Somebody went to a nursery and bought it and transplanted it. It's not for me to say it's nothing—it's something to the person who put it there.'

"It means a lot to me to get paid for the work, but it means just as much to the client that their home is the way they want it to be. They take pride in that. Part of my job is keeping that in mind. Too many people in business—music too for that matter—define pride as 'I know what I'm doing, don't tell me how to do my job.' That's not what I'd call pride. You don't get asked back with that attitude. What's proud about that?

"The easiest thing to do when you're building a business is just tell the truth and back it up. I still don't get why so many people find that hard to understand. Why spend all your time replacing customers when you can keep the ones you have, do good work, make them happy and earn their trust so they call you back again and again? I made sure my sons knew that, every time we went out to work. It doesn't matter what you do, but always exceed people's expectations. Don't just make them happy, make them better than that. Just this week one of my customers paid me in advance for a job in the morning, and left to go to work. Six o'clock rolls around, he comes home and I'm still out there. He says to me, 'Man, you got to be kidding, you mean to tell me I paid you in advance for this and you're still here?' I said, 'Yes, and I'll be back tomorrow until I finish.'

"You want the simplest way to impress someone? Don't cut

corners on yourself or on anyone else. In a time when people get away with just enough, just do it right. My goodness, you gonna run away with a little money just because you can? Think that person is going to hire you back? We were on a job and one of my crew broke a window with the ladder. He wanted to just leave it. I said, 'No, they didn't break that. We did. They're paying us, and you're going to run off?' You can't do that. We'll pay for it or fix it, whichever they want, but you can't just leave your mistakes behind. That person will understand an accident, and they'll call you again if they know you can be trusted. The time will come too when you need people to take your word, and if you have a bad reputation, believe me, there isn't a town big enough to hide in. Word gets around. People hear things. You can get a bad reputation with one poor decision you make in a moment of being too proud. No . . . I was proud to do it right. What I did made me proud, on the air and on the job, not what I could get away with."

He laughs—"I'm probably the only DJ in all of Los Angeles who was up late on Saturday night with James Brown and in church the next morning. I never missed it. The Figueroa Church of Christ was always so good to me. Those people would patronize the businesses that sponsored me and they always listened in. I produced a record of the Church of Christ a cappella choir for them, and I'm as proud of that as I am of anything else I did in music."

THERE'S A long pause at a crosswalk on Western Avenue as Joe drives back toward Baldwin Hills. All the kids on foot and skateboards wear headsets, and the thump of rap comes from the car beside us as we wait for people to cross.

"I guess I might have climbed much higher than I did in the music business," Joe says, "but I had this other business going, and my sons to think about, and I finally got tired of it. That music business ate people up. Lots of people who should have walked away didn't and maybe they should have. All the labels and radio stations wanted to follow the money. I was burned out and the music was taking other directions; by 1965 The Beatles and the British bands had come in, and country rock was starting, and the San Francisco scene was starting up. The little stations got bought up. The little labels disappeared. R&B wasn't around long when you think about it; everything that was different and distinctive about artists like Sam Cooke and The Platters got blended into everything else. It was just too hard to sell a record or rise up in the business here—you'd have to leave town to succeed somewhere else before you could break through in Los Angeles. And I had obligations. I still had my family and the business.

"I'd gone as far as I thought I could go. The 50,000-watt stations didn't have a place for me and I knew that. If I'd been a better reader, maybe I'd have had a chance to rise in the business, I don't know. But I don't regret leaving. This really was the City of Angels in those days, and anything could happen, but walking away wasn't so hard. I had more ahead of me that I wanted to do."

Pride in our family was a commitment, not a reason to pay less attention. You were expected to meet a standard because you were representing the family. You were representing your race, the city, your school—you weren't accountable just to yourself . . . And my pride came from meeting their expectations. I wouldn't ever let them down.

IT IS a rare day when you can catch Larry Massengale, Joe's third son, taking it easy. Today finds him doing his version of relaxing: doing chores in his two-acre ranch in Chatsworth, on the northern edge of the San Fernando Valley. Out here in the foothills of the San Bernardinos, the sidewalks are bridle paths. He and his wife share a big white house with two horses, a llama, two dogs and a family of peacocks.

Among the Massengale brothers, Larry is the most private one and the most like Joe—hardheaded, good-humored, spiritual and independent. For thirty years he has run his own business, Complete Auto Detailing, with clients all over Los Angeles. This afternoon he relaxes in the sun as the horses nibble the grass in the paddock.

As he approaches fifty, Larry is debating with himself about what comes next. "I'm preparing now for the final months of my business, and getting ready to wrap things up here," he says. "My wife and I are building a house in Las Vegas, and when that's ready, I want to take six months off. That'll be a first for me. Time to travel, play golf, just rest and think awhile. Since my early twenties I've had to work just about every single day, so it might be nice to live without a schedule for a while.

"The hard part is that some of my customers are people I've known for twenty, twenty-five years. Can you believe that? They aren't business contacts anymore, they're family. I'm part of their household now. I know their kids. We talk to one another as friends. I actually cried with one of them yesterday. We were reminiscing about things and the tears welled up. When I started working for them I was just a kid with a few bucks to my name. They vested their faith in me and I came through for them. There's a relationship there that goes beyond business. For all these people to be telling me, 'We're going to miss you' . . . that makes it hard for me to walk away."

"My dad's customers had the same loyalty to him. It doesn't happen by accident. There were dozens of businesses just like his here in Los Angeles. There are hundreds just like mine. But I'll tell you, find a business of any kind that actually keeps its word, and that's the one you stay with. So many people you deal with today cut corners and make excuses . . . keeping your word is the simplest way to keep your customers, and it makes me feel great. My father showed me that from day one: your word is your bond. Give people nothing less than that and then some."

The peacocks squawk and the horses roll in the dust as

Larry sits on the steps of the tack shed in his backyard. "I can tell you where that loyalty comes from. When we did land-scaping," he continues, "my dad always told us that the most important job is the cleanup. Anybody can do the trees, but when we were done, the place would be sparkling. It might take me three hours to clean up after a job, but there wouldn't be a twig or a leaf out of place. Everything was clean and wa-tered from the back to the front. People feel pride in their homes and properties, and making them feel that pride gave me mine. It's a practical way to think—let your customers see your higher standard, and then meet that standard again and again. I see nooks and corners inside my customers' cars I know they never see, but *I* see them. The temptation might be there to just get away with what I need to do and let the rest go undetected. But for me it's never good enough, never. I know my work. My customers tell me all the time, 'Larry, okay, *okay*—enough! Don't do any more!' But they've never told me I left the job half done or that it wasn't good enough."

Taking care of the horses helps Larry burn off some of the energy he feels as the day heats up. He feeds, waters and brushes them in their stalls before letting them out again to graze.

"I've never been really satisfied," he says. "Just now, at this age, can I truly say I've gotten comfortable in my own skin. My dad had the things that drove him, like growing up poor, not having shoes to wear. I had mine too. I was uncomfortable with who I was, how I looked and who I was inside. I wasn't sure of my direction in life. But now, getting close to fifty, I've figured out that no decision is a decision. You might as well take a direction and face the consequences—that's part of being a man. So having taken risks with this career all my life, I'm ready for some new ones.

"My brothers will tell you, of all of us, I'm the one who's most like my father. My business is very much like his was, my way of looking at things is pretty close to his. He's a no-nonsense man, and he and I used to butt heads all the time over anything—dating, careers, school. I made him angry many times. I think I remind him of himself a lot. He's not tolerant of his own weaknesses, so he sees mine pretty vividly and he gets right on me. I think it was because he was so sensitive about his own mistakes, and about the things he didn't have, that he was especially sensitive to my mistakes and to the slightest suggestion that I'd take the wrong example from him. He was a perfectionist without being perfect.

"He knew from his childhood in Texas that even an innocent error could be your last one—he saw people die for their mistakes. In the world he knew, if you made a mistake, that was your life. It wasn't that different in mine. The era of lynchings and Emmett Till was when he came of age; in my life it was Watts, a bomb ready to go off in 1965 and again in 1992. That danger is always there. And a sense of foolish pride that tells you you're safe is a deadly invitation.

"Pride in our family was a commitment, not a reason to pay less attention. You were expected to meet a standard because you were representing the family. You were representing your race, the city, your school—you weren't accountable just to yourself. My teachers, my brothers, my dad all expected that of me. And my pride came from meeting their expectations. I wouldn't ever let them down. That's a humbling thing, and the humility of that kind of pride is what I'm talking about . . . checks and balances. Pride and humility. Two sides of the same idea. You'll hear this from all of us."

Larry started landscaping with his father at age six. "Saturdays, Sundays, every summer. Middle-of-the-night jobs in the rainy season and during the Santa Ana winds. It didn't matter if you had a cold or something—if your legs moved, you were out there. I'd watch my dad and I'd be asking, 'Why does this guy do this?' But I understood later on when I became a father myself—the tree business was school, and that was how he taught us to handle life. He was teaching me all the time when I didn't even know it.

"There was no way he'd let you embarrass him on the job. You had to do it right: the uniform, the truck, every aspect of the job. You had to pay attention to the details, every last one. You couldn't do it less than what he wanted. He'd say, 'It's *their* property, but it's *my* job.' And it was about pride, about the right kind of pride shown in the right way. That's the principal lesson he taught me: there are different kinds of pride, and different ways to feel it.

"Both my parents drilled faith in God in us. Do the right thing and trust in God. Second was character—what are you doing when no one is looking? Can you be accountable for who you really are? I've had customers who seem surprised when I find money in their cars and return it to them—in Los Angeles they expect that someone working in their cars will take it instead of giving it back. That's what happens. I make sure my customers know me better than that. My dad did the same for his clients. The work was secondary—anyone can do the work—but honesty and character, being the best you can be at any given time regardless of the task, was the real source of his pride, and it's the same for me.

"Until I was well into college I thought everyone was raised like we were. I guess I ought to have known that most elementary school kids didn't spend afternoons watching the races at Santa Anita. I think the first thing I learned how to read really well was *The Daily Racing Form*," he laughs. "But talking with other people was amazing to me—their families seemed so permissive, the kids getting away with anything, wrecking cars and getting into trouble, and their fathers never said *anything*. My brothers and I got into all kinds of trouble, but I'll tell you, my father was aware of just about everything that was going on in our lives, and you had to know he'd make you accountable for it, just like he was. If he didn't see it, one of the other brothers did, so there was no way you could mess up for long. My father never let us forget that we had to look out for one another. That was one of the foundations of the whole family. Joe Jr. was responsible for Michael, Michael was responsible for me, I looked out for Randy, Randy kept an eye on Patrick. We all look out for Andre. My brothers would never let anything happen to me. My dad made sure of that. He insisted on that, and that meant we'd all keep each other out of trouble. The temptations here in this city were overwhelming, and we worked all the time to keep each other safe not only from bad influences outside but from ourselves."

Larry laughs as he remembers. "Accidents happened—we were boys, and we'd knock each other around all the time, but we couldn't hide it. The worst thing in the world would be to have something happen and know my dad would be home in two hours and saying to each other, 'Oh, man, what are we going to do?' We lived next to a doctor, luckily, and more than once he sewed us up before my dad got home, so the injured party would have to stay under wraps while Dad got cleaned up, but then he'd look around and say, 'Where's Randy?' 'Where's Michael?' Oh, man . . . Randy comes out with a bandage on, and it was, 'What the hell happened?' We always covered for each other, but we never let each other get away with anything. When I got to junior high school, Michael was one of the student body officers. One day things got out of hand in the cafeteria and there was a big food fight, stuff just flying everywhere, kids running around acting crazy, and I thought I'd do it too. I'm running out of the school and there's my brother Michael. He grabs me by the collar and says, 'Get your ass back in that school!' Think of the time—this is the 1960s; we're five Black kids living in a single-parent household; we were exactly the people who were most vulnerable to every pressure and every temptation of the time and the place. People just like us, people we knew, didn't survive the time because they had a moment somewhere, somehow, of making assumptions about their own safety or invulnerability, and that's the other side of pride, isn't it . . . assuming too much. There wasn't any wiggle room with my dad—if you were doing something wrong and he saw it, you heard about it right then and there: 'Dammit, Larry, didn't I tell you—!'

"Nothing got past him. I'd do something bad somehow, and we'd go out on a job and I'd spend the whole day hoping he didn't know about it. We'd work for hours and he wouldn't say a word, and I'd be thinking maybe, just maybe, I'm gonna get away with it this time . . . and then at the end of the day he'd be sitting in the truck with a cigar, arm out the window, looking around perfectly relaxed, and he'd say, 'So, Larry, what's happening with so-and-so . . . ?' And oh, *man* . . ." he says with a laugh. "I'd be *nailed*."

Larry pauses at the llama pen. "A couple of days ago we had some kids from the inner city out here for a visit. Some of those children had never seen animals like these with their own eyes. Never touched a horse, never sat on one. They spent the whole afternoon here."

THE STORY of Larry's car-detailing company sounds much like that of Joe's tree business. "A friend of mine from college got into it and invited me to join him. He was making seven hundred dollars a week, and in 1977 that was good money. He had the idea that we'd start our own business. We nearly starved to death those first couple of years—we'd have five dollars between us and put three dollars' worth of gas in the car, then we'd put on suits and go to a bar holding one of those buffet happy hours. We survived on that food—we'd buy one beer each and then eat a heap of chicken wings.

"It took us probably five or six years to really get the business rolling, and those were some lean years. But you make a choice when you go out on your own. I'd graduated from college and I spent a while in the corporate world. I was the first Black production planner at a big cosmetics company here in L.A., and the only Black guy in management. People told me I was the best thing that ever happened there, and I liked the work. But I started thinking, Wow, this place duplicates effort and loses time and loses money like I've never seen. I thought they'd want ideas, and I was eager to try things, but I got told, 'No, we don't do things like that.'

"Maybe they were right. I was young and they were more experienced, but it was frustrating to offer some common-sense idea that would work and watch it get dismissed. I realized, they weren't dismissing the ideas I had . . . they were dismissing me *having* them.

"Six months in to the position, I was doing really well, but I kept noticing my supervisor, who'd been there for years, come back from lunch a little drunk, and I noticed I started doing the same thing—I'd have a drink at lunch and get a buzz just to cope with the work, and it hit me—what's happening to me? If I let this go on, I'll be just another middle-aged guy drinking at lunch. I ran to the door. It took me years to get back up to the level of income that would have come easily had I stayed, but I saw the price other people paid for that, and it was just too high for me.

"You'd have to be raised in my family to understand how we all feel about being entrepreneurs. It wasn't even a question for us. We've all been in and out of companies, but a full-time job working for someone else was always a temporary condition. If you like that kind of security, more power to you, but staying inside that safe place comes at its own high price, so you might as well follow your heart and do what you really want to do. My dad never had security—his safety net was his character, his pride and integrity. He showed us by example how we could do that. He taught us to be the masters of our own fates, to run our own lives. We were in control of who we are. It has its bumps and bruises along the way but that's what builds character, doesn't it. Just like with furniture, it's those little dings and scratches that give character to an antique. They tell a story. Same with people. You take the opportunities and the hard times and you keep going. It didn't occur to us to do it any other way.

"I'm at the gym at five-thirty until six-thirty, and then I'm on the road to wherever I need to go, Redondo Beach, Beverly Hills, Malibu, the Valley, everywhere. It's tough, yes, but it doesn't bother me because of my upbringing. We worked from one end of town to the other. Today I go all over Los Angeles and know it by heart because of all the places we worked.

"I'll never forget one job. It was just my dad and me out in the desert somewhere east of the city. I was up in the tree and he was on the ground with the pruning pole. I was moving slow as molasses—must have been 115 degrees. I was just exhausted. Barely moving. Very quietly my dad walked under and looked up and said, 'Larry? Ain't nobody gonna walk off the street and do this work for us. So you might as well make up your mind right now to get it done.' I stood there for a moment cursing under my breath, but said to myself, 'He's right, and the quicker I get this done the quicker I can get out of this tree and we can go home.' And I worked like a monster until we were done.

"That's how I am now. Tomorrow's Sunday, and my guys and I are working sunup to sundown. Same as last week, same as next. I wouldn't have it any other way."

As Larry talks, his son Marques works not far away, watering the grass and feeding the peacocks. Marques is an actor and a football player, with one movie under his belt and a contract to play in the NFL Europe. Their relationship gets better as they both get older. It wasn't always this solid. "My father was a master of discipline," Larry says. "He had his moments now and then when he lost it, as anyone does, but all through his upbringing and his days here, he kept his head. I was like that with my son, and he hated it—*hated* it. When he was in high school here in Los Angeles, he was a good-looking, popular kid, star of the football team. He had the world in his hands, and he decided he was going to rebel his last year. He'd disappear on the weekends and not come home at all until Sunday night. He did that for about two months, and one day I'd had enough. I walked up to him—he was standing with all of his friends—and I said, 'You're out of here.' I was going to send him to live with my brother Patrick in Denver. Marques didn't believe that I'd actually do it. That Sunday I had his ticket ready. Everybody was mad, my wife, my daughter, his friends; I mean, he was the quarterback of the team so his whole *school* was angry. But I knew that if I let that pride of his go unchecked, things would go badly for him. No one else was going to confront him. I knew that Patrick, being raised like I was, would do the right thing, would show him something he needed to know. I put him on a plane that afternoon. His mother could barely speak to me—'How could you do this to my son?' He was gone a whole year. Now you see how close we are. We talked about it—he told me, 'You were right, I was headed down the wrong path.' My dad would have done the same thing.

"This is nothing new. My college education focused on politics and history, and I hope I got some perspective from it on who I am and on how to live a life that leaves things better. Running a business or a family isn't so different from leading an army or a family or a nation—those lessons apply. Alexander, David, Napoleon, Hitler—the simplest mistakes of character and arrogance are powerful enough to bring down nations. Imagine what they'd do to my family or my life if I made them too. If you can't control yourself, how are you going to set an example for your family, how are you going to control any aspect of your business or your money?

"There's a practical sense of pride that seems so simple . . . it's understanding when something is truly to your advantage. If it isn't, you shouldn't be doing it. The hard part is understanding that what looks good right now won't be good very soon, doing something that feels great now or leaving a job half-done. Pride can blind you—you tell yourself in that you can't make mistakes; you say, well, it happened to him but it can't happen to me. Pride can make you think you're above all that. Nobody is. Pride without personal self-restraint and integrity? Very, very dangerous. Integrity and character will get you through the times when you don't feel pride, but pride without those two things is something to fear.

"A lot of this has to do with faith, but faith isn't passive. Faith is trusting in God and *doing the work*. It doesn't just happen. This isn't about just expecting things to take care of themselves. When I was growing up, we were up every day at five to wash the truck. My father would stick his head in the door—'Get up!' If it was cold out we'd use hot water, but that was the only concession my dad made about that. We were surrounded by doctors and professionals in that neighborhood, View Park . . . well, by six A.M. we were ready to go out selling. Our friends, doctors' kids, might see us and say, 'Hey, you guys, come to the beach, come play basketball,' and we'd say no . . . They'd laugh at us. We had to work and they didn't.

Years later, we'd hear about some of those same people dying of drug overdoses or suicide. We always had to do our chores—it kept us all on the straight and narrow. My dad would tell us, 'You need to do this because this is what *keeps you livin'*!' "

◼◼◼

THE SKY is dark and the moon is still up as Larry readies his Chrysler van for the day. The back is packed neatly with buckets, hoses, spray bottles, a vacuum cleaner, extension cords and washcloths. His work clothes are well-worn sweats and a baseball cap.

Larry's first stop of the day is a gated mansion on a green street north of Sunset Boulevard in Beverly Hills. He arrives before seven to work for two of his favorite clients, a husband and wife whom he sees every week. They greet him warmly, invite him in for coffee when he's ready, and hand him the keys to their cars. Larry drives a black Mercedes and a white BMW out to the curb and gets to work as the sun comes up.

His routine is always the same. He starts by spraying the tires with a polymer, and then hoses the body down for a thorough scrub with a soft cloth and a soap-wax blend. It's unusual to find him by himself at this. Most days he has one or two crew to help, but this is a relatively light day so he can indulge himself. The sky is cloudless. The trees glow with the morning light.

"I really enjoy it when I work by myself," he says. "Most days I'm out with the crew and we're talking, but when it's quiet like this I can think. I get into a zone . . . I used to watch my father with the pruning pole in his hands, and you could talk with him but he was really in another world. His attention was all on the job, on doing it right. I get the same way—look at this morning, the sky's bright blue, it's cool and quiet, and it's just beautiful here. These clients are friends of mine. I know them well, know their daughter. I'm making them happy. This isn't brain surgery. It's about giving people what they want, making their lives a little easier. Affecting their day in a positive fashion; that's what I value. I feel blessed."

Black cars are a specialty for Larry. It's nearly impossible to get one clean without leaving streaks. He scrubs one side and rinses before moving on, then rubs a chamois over the whole surface to take off every drop of water. He pops the hood and the trunk to clean along the rims, and opens the doors to get the inside panels. "Working with Joe pretty much gave me no choice about being a perfectionist," he says, smiling.

"I don't know if that version of pride is something you can learn by experience, or something that's fed to you from an early age. I'd like to think you can learn it, but it takes more than just the rhetoric to get people to do the right thing. I know they try to teach this in business school and in corporate training, but it takes the right person to hear the wisdom. To me it's second nature. I can't help but think like this. It's an instinct. If you don't have the common sense to see it, I don't really know if it can be taught.

"A lot of people might have just walked away from a business like this and never looked back. They'd get frustrated with the hours and the standards you have to meet to keep customers. I didn't. The pride I take in my work is part of who I am from the early days. I don't want less.

"Here I am washing a car . . . does it sound like too much to say there's a spiritual aspect to it, like there is to any work? To me, the desire to do it right, no matter what you do, is something that becomes who you are, your identity. It needs to be that deep. It changes you. I think my brothers would tell you the same. Living it is a hundred times harder than saying it. But look what you get back.

"Whole industries have been built this way and whole industries have died for misunderstanding pride. They think it's about being able to get away with breaking rules. That's not pride. That's arrogance. My brothers and I learned the difference early from my father. A Massengale doesn't do drugs. A Massengale takes care of himself and his business. A Massengale is a polite person. A spiritual person. He depends on his family and on God. That's what he taught us all. It's not that complicated. You start there and you can do anything. My customers are some very savvy, very successful people. You can't snow someone who did it right. That's the kind of customer I want, the smart ones. They appreciate knowing they're getting a service from someone who thinks like they think. They did it right, and they respect me for doing it right too. That's why we talk as equals, as friends. We know we're the same kind of person. You can't put a dollar sign on that, but I'll tell you, it means a lot to me."

The clients come out to chat. They chide Larry about his impending "retirement," knowing full well how much he likes his work. As they go back inside, Larry mentions that these people are self-made, like a surprising number of people in the neighborhood. The husband is an immigrant who succeeded in import and export; the wife is a former model who worked her way up. Larry's client list is down to about 150 people, and he counts all of them as personal friends.

"You know how it is starting out," he says, wringing the water out of the chamois and resuming. "You need to take anyone who calls. Now I get to choose. I don't advertise at all. I get new clients strictly through word of mouth. If someone sees my telephone number on the van and calls me, I'm pretty good at picking up on who they are. If it's someone I don't feel comfortable with, I probably won't return the call. I have that kind of flexibility now to look for more than money from people. I want the most fulfilling work I can get, and I want to give my best to people who give that back. So I'm not competing anymore for volume."

Online directories list hundreds of auto-detailing companies all over Southern California. On the ride from home this morning, Larry passed three vans like his from other car-care companies. Their approach to the work is different from his. "Yeah, I talk with other guys in the business now and then," he says. "They're amazed at what I charge to do a car. Many of them charge two or three times what I get. The problem they have is that they're constantly turning their business over, churning customers in and out. Nobody likes feeling like they got taken. Overcharge someone once, you lose that customer. And your company has to spend time and money replacing the people you lose. I charge a reasonable price for what I do, and I see many of my clients three or four times every month, so I have no churn at all in a high-turnover business. All my clients are regulars. My overhead is minimal. I have the luxury of taking pride in my work for people I like. And that's what keeps it fun."

The floor mats come out for a scrub with foam cleaner and a stiff brush. Larry leaves them out to air while he sprays the tires again and scrubs them with a new sponge. Once more with the chamois. The finish gleams.

The procedure is the same for the other car. By ten, Larry is coiling his hose and putting away the cloths and bottles to head to his next client.

The drive takes him up over the Hollywood Hills, away from the mansions and gated estates and down into North Hollywood, to a stock-footage company in a stretch of light industry on Burbank Boulevard. The office is lined with movie posters and long shelves of film cans. Larry is a regular here too. He has a bet with the owner: if she loses fifty pounds, he owes her a designer cocktail dress. He hopes to lose.

Her five-year-old silver SUV is parked out back. Larry opens his van and starts the same step-by-step process.

"I WANT people to know me for what I am, with the scars and the mistakes," he says. "My mistakes have been useful to me; they might be useful to someone else, much more than the things I did right. Pride is the truth of who you are, not what you're getting away with. What we learned, I hope, from my dad and from each other is how to keep those checks and balances in ourselves. That's worth more than any false image of flawlessness. Image is meaningless—here in Los Angeles you can manufacture any image you want for yourself regardless of the truth. Image fades; you can't take any pride in it. You need to be proud of the truth, even if it's not so pretty. Nothing in the world is what it seems, and appearances can deceive, including how you appear to yourself. I've known millionaires here who went broke because they started to believe their own press.

"The real story here isn't my life, it's my children's lives. They're the bottom line. Like any father, I want to spoil my kids and give them 'what I didn't have.' But the best thing I can give my son is a truthful example, and hope he can understand both what I did well and what I didn't do well, and how not to make the mistakes I made. They're both college grads; they've never been in serious trouble. What matters most to me is that the next generation of my family gets as much out of hard work and building as my brothers and I got, and as my father got. The ability to build gives you the freedom to try big things, and to fail knowing that you can recover. You do that and you can dream the big dreams. If you're not willing to do the hard things, and endure the failures, you can't dream big. That strength, that will, is the foundation of any greatness you achieve. I know because I tried it the other way. I don't tell my kids things like this because I think I'm better than they are; I say them because I made the mistakes they don't need to make. If I teach them a single thing, I hope it's the difference between being proud and being prideful.

"Pridefulness is a sense of entitlement, of things being inevitable for you, a feeling that you have some sort of a free ride. Anyone can fall prey to that—this isn't about race. Black, White, whoever you are, you make that mistake, and it'll come back to get you. There's no protection against it. Money doesn't undo it, excuses don't. But you can learn from the mistakes made by other people. That's my legacy to them as much as anything else I can pass along. My mistakes might be the most valuable thing I can give my children, because if they listen just once, they can avoid them.

"When my business really got going twenty years ago, I was making a thousand dollars a day. I was still a young man and I was *drunk* with money. I separated from my wife, started dating women; man, I thought I was hot. I was twenty-nine, thirty . . . cars and clothes . . . favorite spots to go in Los Angeles, hanging out with celebrities I was working for. I acted like I owned this city. I thought it was going to last forever. But . . . in all things like that when you have no self-control, it ends. The economy went south. I lost big corporate clients. My marriage was on the ropes and I didn't know what to do. I climbed back up out of that hole one client at a time, and my wife and I fixed our marriage that way, a step at a time. That's what makes this all so sweet now. The mistakes I made were all too common, but the recovery wasn't, and if I hadn't had the family I have, I'd never have gotten back up."

Larry pulls back into the driveway of his ranch. He has a couple hours to put in on the horses and the pets before he can sit back. He's looking forward to both.

"If there's a single thing that comes down to me from my dad, it's as simple as this: you don't just talk about pride, you live it. If you assume that success in life just happens by luck or osmosis or inheritance, you're being falsely proud. Life is work. Being good at it every day is what has made my family proud.

"My dad was a tree trimmer. I'm a car detailer," he says. "I'll take that as a job title. We're two men who dared to bet on ourselves every day for our whole careers. And we won the bet."

LESSON FOUR

PERSISTENCE

Preface by Kent Desormeaux

The bloodlines of every Thoroughbred racing today can be traced to just three horses. Millions of dollars are spent every year to try to perfect the art and science of breeding that perfect animal out of that tiny gene pool, the racehorse that can, as they say, "run a hole in the wind."

The irony is, if they ever get it absolutely right, the whole sport is finished.

If the quality of a horse were just in its genes, we'd have no reason to run the race. We could engineer strength and speed, and you could pick the winner ahead of time, judging by its bloodlines. The real beauty of these animals is that they fool you. Thoroughbreds have personalities just like people (more personality, sometimes). They have moods and quirks. They're smart and competitive and unpredictable. For as much as genetics can tell you, it can't predict which one horse on the track that day will just refuse to give up.

Some of the horses bred for greatness failed because they just didn't have the character it took to win. On the other hand, some of the most honored horses who ever raced looked at first like they might not make it around the track. Seabiscuit, Seattle Slew, Smarty Jones; none of them was the best looking or the biggest at the starting gate. It didn't matter. They all had those qualities of persistence and tenacity *that made them winners. Whatever was missing from their physical makeup, they made up for in sheer will.*

People who love racing call that heart, and you can't find it in a DNA sample. When a million-dollar horse with a pedigree runs beside a long shot with heart, I know which mount I want to be on.

I feel honored to have enjoyed the success I've had in racing, but success isn't in my genes any more than it is in the genes of the horses I ride. The trainers and owners like Joe Massengale who put their confidence in me inspired me with their trust. My friends and associates in the sport gave me their help and support. My mother Brenda taught me my values and morals; my dad Harris gave me a sense of responsibility; my brother Keith helped me hone my competitive skills. Most of all, my wife Sonia and my boys Joshua and Jacob give me the best reasons of all to get back in the saddle and make them proud. For them, I reach down deep to find my own sheer will.

I may not win the next race I'm in, or the one after that, but that won't stop me. Winning is great, but win or lose, the real point is to keep going. The people I love give me heart, and that's why I give my best back to them. Persistence is what I want my sons to get from me: the understanding that life is one long race, and the real victory is that at the end of it, we can look back and know we never quit.

The youngest jockey ever to win 3,000 races and the youngest to win 4,000, Kent Desormeaux is a two-time winner of the Breeders' Cup, the winner of the Kentucky Derby in 1998 and 2000 and the winner of the Preakness in 1998. He was inducted into the National Museum of Racing and Hall of Fame in 2004.

WHEN I joined my brothers out here in the landscaping business in 1947," Joe explains, "we'd go north as far as San Francisco and south almost to Mexico looking for work. You'd have to do that sometimes if things were dry here in Los Angeles. Just get in the truck and go. I still feel like I know every tree in California personally. We didn't know if we'd find jobs or not, but if there wasn't anything going on here at home, we'd have to take our chances out of town. That's hustling—you don't wait for the work to come to you. You go get it.

"We didn't know anything about the Yellow Pages or about advertising ourselves, so we'd just drive up and down the streets, knocking on door after door. We didn't even have a business license. We'd put a ladder on the truck and go west from L.A. out into Ventura, make enough to stay overnight, and then head north into Santa Maria and Monterey and hustle jobs there. We'd get a room if we could find one. We might come back the next day, we might not; sometimes we'd just keep driving. In some of those towns we would do all right, and we'd make enough to keep going. Couple of jobs a day would get you all the way up to San Francisco, and we'd work all over the Bay. San Jose, Salinas, Santa Cruz.

"We might be out hustling work on the road two weeks at a time. I was the high man. My brothers would send me forty feet up a palm tree on a wooden ladder with a saw in one hand and no safety belt. It doesn't get much more dangerous than that. One slip and that would have been it.

"It sounds like a hard life, but it was what we had, and it's like anything else. You got to get out there and hustle just to stay with it. You stop, and the wolves eat you up."

Joe tells this story as he leaves his house on a gray morning for a day at the races at Hollywood Park. Being a little preoccupied, Joe seems not to notice a broken soda bottle in the street as he gets into his pickup. A horse named Holy Bully is running seven furlongs in today's second race. Expectations are low. The jockey is an apprentice running beside five more-experienced riders, including the 1989 Kentucky Derby winner Patrick Valenzuela. Holy Bully came in fourth in his last outing, seven furlongs at Del Mar just like today's race, after starting strong and weakening at the end. The program mentions that the horse has no wins in seven starts. The odds are listed at 10–1. If the race goes as the handicappers expect it to, Holy Bully should finish dead last.

Joe has money on the race. He owns Holy Bully.

THE OWNER sticker on the windshield of his pickup gets Joe a spot close to the Hollywood Park entrance. Every attendant in the lot knows him. All of them call him by his first name and ask how his horse will run today.

Joe attended his first horse race in 1947 with his brother

Bob, a regular player who often came home broke. "I wasn't much of a gambler myself," Joe says as he enters the track. "I played a little now and then, but I had a family and I worked too hard to earn what I had to lose it at places like this. I just liked the sport. And those animals . . . I love the horses, always have. You grow up around horses like I did, and you can spot the intelligence in them. Thoroughbreds are some of the smartest animals you can find. You can see it in their eyes. And when they come around the stretch and it's anybody's race, those silks are flying and the crowd's on its feet . . . man, there's nothing in the world like that."

Even a relatively modest track like Hollywood Park displays plenty of the rich history of racing. This facility dates from 1938, when some of the great names of the movie business built themselves a playground. The gardens outside are immaculate year-round, blooming with flowers and green hedges. The infield sparkles, a manicured park with rolling turf, fountains and ponds inside the two-mile track.

A good horseman knows to watch carefully before he invests. Joe Massengale watched the sport in places like this for twenty years before he bought in, observing the horses and the owners, asking questions and remembering what he was told.

"I used to stand by the winner's circle at my favorite track, Santa Anita. Imagine me, a kid with a couple of dollars in my pocket, taking the old Red Cars twelve miles from Los Angeles City College to Santa Anita to watch the races. Things were different back then. It was a lot more Big Mes and Little Yous, you know? The people racing horses were like dynasties. That track would bring in the elite owners and mounts from all over the United States, the bluegrass owners from Kentucky,

Calumet Farms, the Vanderbilts, the big stables from the very wealthy families back east.

"Most days I didn't bet. I just wanted to watch the horses and to watch the people. They got me thinking. I'd see the owners in the boxes and the winner's circle, dressed so beautifully, looking so happy. They just looked like they had everything they could want. I didn't have much, but I asked myself, 'Why can't I do that?'

"Most people don't think about owning horses—it's a major financial outlay, and it's a dangerous game in many ways. In every race you see, there's an ambulance on the track following the field. That tells you something right there about how hazardous it can be. Anyone who underestimates the jockey as an athlete doesn't know this sport; those people take risks an average person would never even try. And owners can lose a fortune in a moment. I've seen a horse that was going to sell for thirty million dollars and the owners said, 'We'll run him one more time before the sale.' That horse stepped in a hole on the track and broke its leg and had to be put down right there. Tragic. That's the risk to riders and horses both.

"So there I was, a working man with a family, and I wanted to get in. I didn't see it as a gamble. I looked at it like I looked at my business. I watched and learned. I listened when people talked to me and I asked lots of questions. If I could learn something by mucking out a stall, I did it. And I didn't think like a horse player—I thought like an owner before I owned. A horse player is at the track every day, gambling and hoping to win. You do that and you're going to lose. An owner is patient. I didn't buy in until I was fifty years old and felt I was prepared. I had the patience to hang in there and wait for it.

"For me, it was another way to show people what I could do. I wanted people's respect, whatever I did. I knew I could earn it. And I always liked the idea of getting my name out there—you know, I still go back to Marshall, Texas, in my mind. The way I was treated, the way I came up as a kid, no shoes, always hungry, people laughing at me and my family for being poor . . . well, I remembered that. I wasn't trying to be vengeful about it; I just had a point to prove. But you have to be careful. Anger can make you act in haste. You bet too big, you overdo it, and you lose. I knew I could do what I saw lots of people at the track doing, being foolish with money and betting too big and losing it all; or I could use my anger as a motivator, and let it make me resilient. I took my time and enjoyed learning, and that was what I wanted.

"You want to succeed in racing?" he asks. "The smart way is to pay attention, stay honest and have faith to hang in there."

THE CROWD at Hollywood Park is light as he enters. Joe's presence is recognized by friends and players in the stands, by the folks working at the food concessions and the ticket windows. Bettors try to shake a tip on the race from him, as though a man running a 10–1 shot might have a secret weapon.

"The sport of kings," racing is called, and it is literally true. One of the oldest contests on earth, horse racing was featured in the first Olympics in Greece. The raceways of ancient Rome remain visible today all over Italy and the former Roman Empire. It was a passion for the nobles of Britain as early as the Crusades, when the warring knights brought Arab chargers back from the East. The monarchs of England made it a household pursuit. It became a profession under Queen Anne at the beginning of the eighteenth century. Queen Elizabeth II is one of the sport's most conspicuous enthusiasts. The Jockey Club, founded in 1750, still controls British racing.

Thoroughbred racing predates American independence in the New World by more than a century. The first track on this continent is thought to date from 1665. The founding of the American Jockey Club in 1894 organized the country's leading owners to root out the unregulated crookedness in the game. It survived an anti-gambling movement in the early twentieth century to become one of the most popular spectator sports in the country.

The royalist aspect of racing applies as much to the animals on the track as it does to the owners who buy them. Thousands of Thoroughbreds run in the United States and Britain every day, and the bloodline of every one of them can be traced back more than three hundred years to just three horses—the Byerly Turk, the Godolphin Arabian, and the Darley Arabian. These first three were imported from the East to Britain starting in the late eighteenth century and mated with native war horses to produce an unprecedented combination of speed, strength and stamina.

The object of the centuries of selective breeding that followed these Foundation Sires was simply to build the perfect champion. The belief that the qualities of a winner can be captured in the bloodline is why, in any given race, the pedigrees of the horses on the track are better known than the family histories of the people in the stands. Hundreds of millions of dollars change hands every year as owners attempt to breed the drive and muscle that made legends out of War Admiral or Secretariat or Affirmed. And while the money is often well spent, many horses bred for greatness at high expense simply don't fulfill their promise. It has been proven again and again that something intangible in the spirit of a great horse doesn't show up on a bloodline chart. Many of the most revered animals in racing history looked like losers on paper. The legendary Seabiscuit was a mean-tempered, knock-kneed runt picked up for $7,500 by a trainer with a hunch who turned him into the 1938 Horse of the Year. Seattle Dancer sold for $13,100,000 in 1985, a record, and returned just $152,413, while his clumsy, unimpressive half-brother went for $17,500 and won $1,208,726 in purses, including a Triple Crown: Seattle Slew.

Because the stakes are so high, the "kings" in American Thoroughbred racing have generally been the owners who could afford to lose big money: heirs, industrial magnates, athletes and big-ticket entertainers like the ones Joe Massengale watched so closely as a kid.

It is very likely that Joe's horse Holy Bully is the only Thoroughbred running this afternoon whose owner made a career of manual labor. Today, the horse works. Tomorrow, the owner will.

BEFORE THE race, the horses are led around the Walking Ring in the garden outside the Hollywood Park track. It's a chance for people to see these magnificent, moody animals up close.

An experienced horseman learns to read a horse's frame of mind, and often sees right here how this race might go. "I had an eye for when a horse was skittish or worried," Joe says as he watches them. "You can see it in the way they carry themselves, just like you can observe what's happening in a person's mind by how they behave. These horses know they're in competition. If a horse is perspiring or skittish, that horse is nervous. We call that 'mustangin'.' That's not a good sign. Some horses look cool and ready, and that's encouraging. The warm-up tells you a lot. Are they jumpy? Does the jockey need to call a lead horse over to help them settle down? Do they hesitate getting into the gate? The good horses seldom act up like that. You can tell they're focused. They want to run."

Holy Bully is a big chestnut stallion with a sixteen-year-old apprentice, Alex Bisono, in the saddle. Apprentices are called "bug boys" because their names come with an asterisk in the program to show they are new in the racing game. This race is a "maiden claimer," meaning that none of the horses has won, and all of them are up for sale. Quartez, the favorite, is a 2–1 bet. Trail Striker is 3–1. The rest are 4–1, 7–1, 5–1, except for Joe's horse, the lowest.

Alex Bisono comes over wearing Joe's light blue–dark blue checkered silks with a red JM on the front and back, and promises to run his mount hard for the $21,000 purse.

Joe heads back to the stands. He stops to place a bet for luck on his own horse, a leap of faith considering the odds. In Holy Bully's last race, the horse started strong but drifted to the outside of the field and weakened in the last leg, finishing out of the money. No one, Joe included, expects much from the animal today. Holy Bully is up for grabs as a "claimer."

Today's race is more or less an audition for sale to anyone who wants to buy the horse, and Joe hopes to sell and break even.

"The first time it crossed my mind to buy in was 1978," Joe says. "Business was good and I had a little money to invest. I got an emergency tree job from one of my regular clients, a woman I'd known for years. She was from a wealthy family. They were serious owners and breeders in racing, and her husband was a trainer. I was working to cut down a tree limb that fell on her house, and I told her I'd like to become an owner myself. She said, 'Why don't you come to a sale with me and look over some of the horses?' I was able to trade landscaping work at her house and her ranch for shares in my first horses.

"There's a lot to learn. You need to be educated about the breeding and the pedigree, and you have to read the animal as it walks and runs to see if it's sound. Many of them aren't the prototypical elegant Thoroughbred. Some look like they couldn't ever win. But if you're observant, you get an eye for an animal and a feel for its heart. Some horses run ugly. They'll come out of the gate last. But something in them drives them to circle the whole field and win. If it was just in the genes, this would be easy. The truth is, you don't know what a horse is going to do until that starting gate opens."

More people say hello to Joe as he makes his way to a box overlooking the finish line.

"As a small owner, one advantage I have is that my reputation is as good as you can get. Personal reputation is the key. All the money in the world won't buy you back the trust you need if you do somebody wrong at the track. You get a bad name around here, and nobody wants to be bothered with you. Everyone knows everyone else, and things happen fast, on handshakes. There's no time to negotiate. You find out overnight if the jockey you want will be available to ride for you. If people don't trust you, word gets around and you can't get a rider. People have told me I have more friends in the backstretch than anyone. They know I can be trusted, being a gentleman; and being a Black owner, people recognize me. So I treat people as I hope they'll treat me.

"I like earning people's respect. And I like upholding the good name of the sport. Some people give it a bad reputation, but it's a business and it protects its interest like any business. The effect of bad rumors is even greater scrutiny—if a jockey pulls up for no reason on the stretch; if a jockey doesn't push a horse that's a clear favorite; then I promise you, that rider will be in the track office. The stewards don't care who you are—if your rider or your horse does the wrong thing, you're coming down. They'll suspend you in a second. There's no prejudice in the stewards' office. They don't care whose horse it is, small owner, big stable, Black or White—if something isn't right, they're all over it. And the stakes are so high—can you imagine a trainer or a jockey with a career to protect trying to influence a race and blowing it all for just one win? That's foolish, and this isn't a foolish business. You lose your good name here and your career's over. I admire everyone who's spent a lifetime working and training and learning so they can compete at this level. I like being accountable that way myself.

"I knew a jockey here from Aqueduct who was out here to ride, who was just seen—*seen*—in the company of some gamblers, and the stewards suspended his license to ride on this coast, and then back east, and that was it. His career was over. He never rode again. I don't work with the kind of people who'd do things wrong. My dad was the kind of man who'd walk fifteen miles to return fifty cents he owed a man. I'm never going to put that at risk myself and I've never let anyone who worked for me do that. Mess around and you won't last, and, man, life is a race. It doesn't matter what you do. Business, family . . . there's no such thing as a short run. I got into this sport with my good name, and that's what I'll have when I leave it. I worked hard to get here, and I'm in this race for the whole two miles."

A BLACK owner in Thoroughbred racing is remarkably rare. A few entertainers and athletes such as M.C. Hammer and Berry Gordy have raced with some success, but at every level, the racing game has historically been one of the most racially segregated sports in the United States. Fifteen of the first twenty-eight jockeys to win the Kentucky Derby were Black, starting with Oliver Lewis in 1875. Isaac Murphy, the first to win Derbys back-to-back and winner of 44 percent of the races he rode in, is still considered one of the greatest of all time. But when Marlon St. Julien rode a 50-to-1 long shot named Curule in the 2000 Kentucky Derby as a last-minute entry, he was the first African-American in seventy-nine years in the saddle in the Run for the Roses.

Of course there is no formal policy about the race of a jockey—all that matters to an owner or, more important, to a horse, are skill and weight. Joe considers only those things himself in seeking a rider for his mounts. Still, it disturbs Joe and many racing historians that the early contributions of Blacks to the sport have not been recognized. Writer Edward Hotaling calls African-American jockeys "our first professional athletes." But after such an auspicious beginning, African-Americans virtually disappeared from racing after the turn of the century, finding themselves denied licenses by the prestigious Jockey Club, and largely vanishing even from the supporting roles.

Joe Massengale didn't ask for permission to join the sport, and he didn't let the question of race get in his way here any more than he did anywhere else. "I got into it when I had the cash flow. That was the main issue. I knew I could take a few losses and keep going. And at fifty years old, I knew enough to make mistakes and not second-guess myself. I know people who knocked themselves down for years because they sold a horse that blossomed or lost an opportunity. You can't allow yourself to 'woulda-coulda-shoulda' like that. That's worse than losing. Losing happens. But beating yourself down doesn't make it better. I just took it slow and hung in. Going after too much too fast is a mistake. A career in racing is the same as a single race—you come out of the gate too fast and you take the lead for a while, but if you don't have some kick in the stretch, other horses will pass you by.

"As far as any racial issues went, well, people have their way of thinking and I have mine. One time I got questioned by a security guard at Del Mar. This man had a hard time believing that a Black man in a pickup truck was an owner, and he kept insisting I was parking in the wrong place. He said a couple of things I didn't appreciate and I lost my temper. I got out of the truck and tossed my Owner credential on the ground and promised I'd never return to that track. But this is a small world, and it polices itself closely. Word gets around if something isn't right. *The Daily Racing Form* reported it as an incident, and the track stewards called me in to account for myself. I told them what happened and they understood. They didn't impose a fine on me, but they still asked me to apologize to the attendant, and I just flatly refused. The Chief Steward took me aside and said, 'Joe, listen to me—haven't you worked too hard to let your temper get the best of you like that? You had a long haul to get to where you are, how are you going to let a man who doesn't know half what you know to make you that mad?' They weren't saying he was right; they just said an owner is expected to conduct himself appropriately. You can't let people step on you, but I had to admit, the Chief Steward had a point. I shouldn't have let a man who was that ignorant make me so angry."

The horses are led around the clubhouse turn toward the starting gate across the track. The bugler rises and trumpets the traditional "Call to Post" as the tote board adjusts to record the last few bets.

EVEN A casual racing fan would recognize some of the greatest jockeys ever to ride in the racing photos Joe has at home: Willie Shoemaker, four times the winner of the Kentucky Derby, three times the Preakness winner and five times the winner of the Belmont Stakes, rode Joe's very first winner, Atom Eyes, at Santa Anita in 1981. (For Shoemaker, Joe broke his own rule: he asked the great jockey for an autograph.) Chris McCarron rode over seven thousand winners and won over a quarter of a billion dollars in purses. He brought Dove In Flight home in first place for Joe here at Hollywood Park in 1985. Kent Desormeaux won on Gourmet Girl for Joe at Hollywood Park in 1997.

Joe's most treasured win was his biggest, the 1998 Bay Meadows Oaks. Mention the horse's name and Joe still smiles.

"Gourmet Girl ... beautiful black filly, long legs ... I remember the first time I saw her with my partner. I said, 'That's the one I want.' Bay Meadows is up north in San Mateo, in the same area where my brothers and I used to work on those long trips away from home. Imagine how that felt ... fifty years after I was up there hustling for work so I could pay twenty-five cents to get back over the Bay Bridge, I had a horse at Bay Meadows for the biggest race of my life.

"That track was a beautiful place, and a stakes race like the Oaks is a big event. The track rolled out the red carpet for the owners that day. My horse didn't get much respect from the newspapers. Most of the horses were local favorites, and the Bay Area papers were all saying that a horse called Nonies Dancer looked like the one to beat at 3–5 odds. One of the sportswriters called Gourmet Girl a 'shipper,' meaning a horse shipped in for the race from out of town. They thought she might finish in the money, but never in first place.

"I was up there for the race with my brother Oliver. The night before the Oaks, I was just pacing the hotel room. Couldn't close my eyes. I kept reading the *Racing Form* over and over like there was something in there I didn't know already. And I just got a feeling. I woke my brother up and told him, 'Oliver, we're going to win. We're going to take this by ten lengths.' He rubbed his eyes and asked me, 'How do you know?' I just did—I never felt anything so strongly in my life as that. I just knew it.

"I couldn't watch the race. I sat in the clubhouse. You see how it is here, people from all over the track come up and talk and I like that, but this time I just wanted to be by myself. I watched it on television. I'll never forget it—they opened the gate and I heard the announcer say, 'Gourmet Girl stumbles to her knees!' I just said a prayer. Roberto Gonzales was riding. He pulled her back up. She got back on her feet and, man, she moved. She ran into second place behind Reign on Rainer. At the far turn, she just poured it on and took the lead. Five lengths, ten lengths . . . they said it was twelve lengths at the end, but I swear it was fifteen. You couldn't see any other horses on the track when Gourmet Girl crossed the finish line. The favorite finished fourth. Seven furlongs in a minute and forty-three seconds.

"Man, I was sixty-eight years old. I walked down that long, long set of stairs to the winner's circle, and I'll tell you, I just couldn't hold back the tears. I'd been up there as a kid working in people's yards for ten dollars a tree, and now, I was a winner in the biggest race of my career. I tried to tell the press how long it took me to win, but I don't know if they really understood . . . fifty years of waiting. Fifty years. But I got to the winner's circle."

The horses tramp and snort into the starting gate at Hollywood Park. The bell rings and the gate flies open and they're off. The pack stays tight for the first two furlongs on the far stretch, and it's impossible to tell Seasonal King from Quartez from Banco de Oro, but you can pick out Joe's blue-and-blue silks in the middle of the thunder. They come around the far turn and start to separate. Holy Bully drops back, running on the outside four lengths behind Quartez in the lead. Four furlongs, five, and then Holy Bully picks it up. The distance to the leader closes. Now it's three lengths.

Joe stands up.

Willie Shoemaker summed up racing in a single sentence: "There are one hundred and ninety-nine ways to get beat, but only one way to win: get there first." Alex Bisono pulls the horse wide on the stretch turn and everyone in the stands can see it: he's moving up. Something drives Holy Bully on as they come around, and the horse gains yard by yard even though it's running wide around the turn. In the home stretch the jockey pours it on, and Joe yells, "Go, go, *go!*" as the 10–1 long shot takes the lead and comes in first by five lengths.

Even before he makes it to the bettors' window, Joe gets handshakes and pats on the back from players and workers at the track. He makes no display of it, but every handshake has a little payoff for the other person. If you didn't bet on Holy Bully today, the owner shares his winnings with you anyway.

After he collects his money, Joe continues touring the track, visiting the restaurants, making sure to talk with girls working the telephones and the elevator operators, and with player after player. Everyone shares his luck, twenty dollars here, fifty there. The money Joe won on his horse at the window is gone by the time he makes it down to the parking lot. Joe tips the attendants big.

THE UNFORGETTABLE 1938 match race between War Admiral and Seabiscuit pitted racing royalty against a tenacious underdog in a contest much like Joe Massengale's career in racing.

The Admiral, tall and sleek, was a wire-to-wire winner in all three Triple Crown races in 1937, and the son of Man o' War, one of the greatest horses of the century. Seabiscuit was short, stocky, a "shipper" brought in from the West Coast, older than War Admiral and with a mixed history. The blood and the odds favored the big horse, winner take all.

The race riveted the nation and still stands as a landmark in the sport. The great writer Grantland Rice described the finish. "The race, they say, isn't to the swift," he wrote. "But it is always to the swift and the game. It so happened that Seabiscuit had these two important qualities in deep abundance. War Admiral could match neither flying feet nor fighting heart. Man o' War's brilliant son hung on with all he had until it came to the big showdown—to the point when the hard-way Thoroughbred, the horse from the wrong side of the track, began really to run."

It was Seabiscuit by three lengths.

"There's nothing like that feeling," Joe says as he pulls back into his driveway. "It really is the sport of kings." Then the biggest winner of the day at Hollywood Park goes inside, comes out with a broom and sweeps up the glass from the broken bottle in the street.

I'm building a company. I'm building it from scratch in a downturn in the sector I'm working in. It's a tough way to get started. You could say I have all the excuses I need for failing. But thinking about my father and what he taught me gets me up and going at five and into the gym at six and here at Spinoza by seven to start on that project that looked too big for me the day before.

SPINOZA TECHNOLOGY occupies a third-floor office in an angular tower in downtown Seattle, with a view of the Space Needle and the Monorail from the front door. Most of the other tenants in the building are law firms and medical companies. Not long ago, these were typical premises for startups in the software industry, but ever since the market crashed, nothing about the software business is typical.

The dot.com and computer boom of the 1990s witnessed a wave of innovative startup companies and created instant fortunes built around unprecedented products and programs. Personal computers and the Internet became part of everyday life as the world was wired with satellite communications and fiber optics. Wall Street responded with an historic bull market and trillions of dollars in venture financing to feed the seemingly insatiable market for new hardware, software and content. Overnight millionaires were as common as the initial public offerings announced every day.

The boom peaked in March 2000, and when the bubble burst, the damage was colossal. The NASDAQ Composite Index, the preferred stock market for technology companies like Spinoza, lost 78 percent of its value. Hundreds of companies in offices just like this up and down the coast from Seattle to San Diego disappeared, taking with them countless jobs and the paper fortunes of the newly rich.

Randy Massengale, Joe Massengale's fourth son, spent thirty years as an executive with some of the most successful firms in the technology field—Tektronix, Intel, Fluke, Microsoft and InfoSpace. Randy incorporated Spinoza in the fall of 2000. Starting a technology company just a few months after the market crashed was like steering a rowboat toward a hurricane. He never hesitated.

The Spinoza office is spartan, with scuffed plain walls and furniture from a warehouse store. Randy's own space is just like the four others in the suite, a pale box with fluorescent lights; the kind of sensory-deprivation chamber that a bigger company might give to an engineer just out of school in hopes that he'll work overtime for a promotion into a more habitable place. A necktie hangs down from a hook on the wall, in case of a fashion emergency (people in this business are more likely to wear white socks than ties). Randy's desk is a drift of papers. The whiteboard is covered with diagrams and lists. The rest of the Spinoza suite is a kitchen with Chinese take-out menus tacked to the walls, a conference room with projectors, two long tables and screens and a lab with racks of hard drives and servers.

During the boom years, software companies looked like toy stores, with Foosball tables, regular pizza deliveries and twenty-year-old executives Rollerblading in the hallways. Spinoza has the minimum required to run the company without comforts, not even a receptionist. The founder of the company answers his own phone. For the first five years since he opened the doors in 1999, Randy took no outside money. Every penny went from his pocket back into the company.

The company has six full-time staff, mostly young guys in jeans and sneakers who eat lunch at their desks. Turnover has been a problem from time to time because Randy is such an effective mentor that people get hired away by the big companies. He and his staff are busy readying Spinoza for an upcoming presentation in Singapore to one of the world's largest computer manufacturers. Randy goes from there to the Gulf States to seek venture capital. This trip is the culmination of years' commitment and building.

After a career with the leading companies in the field, Randy might easily have joined many of his former colleagues and retired in his mid-forties. People he used to work with own professional sports teams as hobbies. Instead, Randy dug back in and started over, aiming not only to succeed even more than he already had, but to demonstrate that he could compete and win as an entrepreneur. Spinoza is developing software for wireless networked audiovisual devices in homes and offices. His customers and deal partners include some of the leading hardware and software companies in the technology industry.

"There are lots of things I got from my dad that I use every day," Randy says, leaning back in his chair. "One key thing is persistence—my dad was persistence personified. If things went wrong, he persisted. If things went right, he persisted.

"I teach a graduate business course called Extraordinary Leaders at Seattle University. It profiles the leadership qualities of accomplished people in politics, business and science. And I really didn't understand how extraordinary Joe Sr. was until I started teaching that course. One of the things I found with exceptional people is that no matter what happens, they *use* it.

"I tell this all the time to my students: there are two things you can do with setbacks, and you see this in the character of every true leader: negatives that you experience in life either go in the 'trunk' or they go in the 'tank.' If they go in the trunk, you carry them around as a burden. They weigh you down and you have to drag them when you move. If they go in the tank, they're fuel. Sometimes a terrible obstruction can become a very powerful fuel. It can drive you to reach your goal. With my father, all his experiences have gone in the tank, even the negative ones, whether they were something to do with his business, or a family member on hard times, or something that happened to him directly—everything has motivated him to keep going.

"That's what I learned from him. My persistence enables me every day to say, Hey, things didn't go well today but it's going to motivate me to do even better tomorrow. It's a very simple idea. Maybe it's a cliché. But if you live it, if you see it in action, it's amazing."

The upcoming appointment in Singapore illustrates his point. "Getting a chance to present to a potential client like this might take six months. I had a business development executive here on staff before, and he's the one who initiated the conversation with them. It took weeks just to get their attention, and at the time, they weren't ready to talk. He got disillusioned and left. After a few months, I called them back myself and said, 'Hey, we need to restart our discussion.' Now they were ready. We met them in Las Vegas to give them a special presentation, and that got the door open for us in Singapore. After years of development work, months of frustration and a lot of plain dogged effort, we're on the brink of a breakthrough."

The whiteboard in the conference room has a to-do list for the trip that might have come straight from Joe's Expert Tree Service:

1. HAVE A BULLETPROOF PRODUCT
2. DYNAMITE PRESENTATION
3. PROFESSIONAL PRESENCE
   - COLLATERAL WELL-WRITTEN AND LAID OUT
   - DRESS WELL, LOOK SHARP
   - KNOW YOUR STUFF: BE PREPARED FOR TWENTY QUESTIONS

Randy and his people go over it point-by-point at a staff meeting that afternoon. They walk through the demonstration they'll give, challenging each other with questions and concerns. Everyone in the room is well aware of the headlines in that day's paper: a major computer hardware manufacturer has just fired its own chairman, and the long-term outlook for technology companies remains scary. There are some tense exchanges. Randy asks more questions than he answers, respecting that the engineers who work for him probably know the nuts and bolts better than he does. The strategic vision, though, comes from him. At the end of three hours, he tells them, "Okay, we've done enough. I have a direction for where we're going now."

WHEN SPINOZA was just getting started, Randy told his chief software architect what he had in mind: he wanted to control hardware such as projectors, screens, audio speakers and DVD players with a cell phone or a PDA. The architect listened, looked blank and said, "Why?"

The answer, Randy knew, lay in Metcalf's Law, one of the commandments of the technology industry. First articulated by an early pioneer in the field, Metcalf's Law states that the value of a network increases in proportion to the square of the number of nodes on the network. People, hardware—whatever makes up that network, the more you add in, the more useful and powerful every element in the network becomes. All these projectors, screens and other devices in Randy's conference room used to work separately, speaking different software languages, using different cables and plugs, requiring experts to use and maintain them. The disunity is an expensive, confusing obstacle. Randy wants to turn them all into a network, with all these devices communicating on a single standard.

He demonstrates using a $99 smart phone and his company's software. He drops both screens, turns on the projector, fires up the DVD player and a laptop and runs a PowerPoint from the palm of his hand while walking around the room. He can change slides in the presentation, zoom, adjust the sound, play or freeze-frame the DVD, all without a hard-wired connection or a laser pointer.

It's cool, but cool alone isn't enough after the crash. Even as the market struggles to come back to life, hundreds of firms are scrambling to capitalize. As Spinoza prepares to pitch in Singapore, the industry media are covering about seventy-five other software startups gathered at the fifteenth annual DEMO technology conference in Arizona. The presentations will show off "a hyper-fast blogging service that lets people publish photos or text on the Web in less than a minute," and "a Web service that generates custom e-mail messages designed to cheer, delight and entertain friends, based on profiles users fill out about intended recipients," and "software that automates travel booking online and integrates results with other desktop programs, such as calendars and spreadsheets." These companies have to dazzle venture capitalists, who by this time have seen every kind of bloatware, vaporware and digital doodad people can think up. Each hopeful entrepreneur gets six minutes to talk. That's a lot—four hundred other companies didn't make it into the room.

Randy points out that the same inexpensive phone in his hand could control hardware not only here, but Spinoza-powered networked devices anywhere—in the building or in the world. He could be standing in Seattle and running this presentation in New Delhi: Metcalf's Law at work. Enabling a company to use and maintain a network like this might well be of substantial value indeed.

"That 'why?' was a reasonable question for my architect to ask," Randy says. "'If it ain't broke don't fix it' is a pervasive attitude. It seems like common sense, and lots of companies work that way. But truth is, that mindset used in the wrong place kills companies. In my industry you have to say, 'If it ain't broke, look harder.'

"Technology is about conceiving solutions for problems other people haven't recognized. We got out in front of this idea two years before anyone else thought of it as an opportunity. Those early years were some tough times, but that effort earned us a lead that puts us ahead of the competition. They have to climb the same learning curve we did, and they're months behind us, and we're accelerating. Soon we hope to be established as the gold standard in our niche.

"Lots of people would have asked 'Why?' But someday soon people will wonder how anyone could have worked effectively without all these devices communicating in sync. When your whole house is made of efficiently linked devices, and you don't need to go downstairs or to another room to turn off your lights or the stereo—or even be in the same country to make sure they're off. When your toaster tells you your toast is ready, it'll be because the toaster has our software. When your kid is home playing a video game instead of studying and the video game sends you an e-mail and you can shut it off from work, you'll thank Spinoza. We're aggregating devices that right now are unaware of each other's existence, and turning them in to a united, simple network that you can control easily."

Randy brings up the program's diagnostics screen. The Spinoza program reads the status of all the devices in the room. It could do the same for networked devices thousands of miles away.

"We're defining quality as ease of use, convenience, even fun to use, and that's why I go home from this feeling stimulated, not bored or tired," he says. "I feel charged about what we're doing. And the time to start was at the bottom of the market, when the whole tech industry was on its back. The collapse of tech stocks made a lot of investors look elsewhere for opportunities. Now it's time again for a new breakout of technology advancements and companies like this. Where do people think that's going to happen? In convergence. In the unifying and simplifying of all these different technologies, in getting all of them to work together in ways that make them all easier to use, more reliable and with a better return. That's our company tag line—'Simplify. Unify.'"

The other company slogan is "All things excellent are as difficult as they are rare," a quotation from the company namesake. Baruch de Spinoza was a seventeenth-century Portuguese-Dutch philosopher who was excommunicated from the Jewish community for his assertion that God and the mechanisms of nature were one and the same. Randy views Spinoza's paradigm of unity in nature as being like his company's vision of the unity of the wired and the wireless. He also appreciates anyone who can swim against the tide.

"I spent my own money for a year researching technology convergence with nine consultants," he remembers. "I filed for a patent in 2000 for intellectual property that's central to our plans for Spinoza. My attorneys told me the filing would take eighteen months. I spent so much on it, they were calling me, saying, 'Randy, are you sure you want to spend any more on this?' I was committed—I told them, 'Keep filing it, find a way.' I was exhausted by the process, but I wasn't about to give up. What's the point of quitting halfway? And too many people do just that. My dad was in business hour-by-hour, day after day, and he didn't give himself the option to quit. He had to draw pretty deep on his inner resources when the outer ones weren't there for him, but he had faith in himself and in God and he never stopped.

"Yeah, I've been tempted sometimes to cut my losses and get out of a risky market, but I remember that he told us all the time that life's all about risk, so you might as well do what you truly want to do. And once you make some progress, people will perceive less risk and they'll want to get in behind you. Trust that—people want to bet on the horse that leads as it goes into the stretch. You might not see it yourself when you turn a corner, but people will be looking to capitalize on the opportunity you create. That's where we are right now. We'll be raising venture funding soon now that the heavy lifting has been done. And it's sweeter to have run the long race, like my dad's career in racing. He waited twenty years to buy in and years longer to become a major winner. I can promise you that victory was a sweet one for him, and I want that feeling myself."

IN 1999, new companies needed only to describe themselves as high-tech or Internet-related to secure investment capital.

In 2000, even the soundest business plans could go unfunded as skittish investors avoided the whole technology market. New business development slowed to a crawl.

Add to these obstacles one particular to Randy and a handful of other entrepreneurs and executives: Blacks make up 13 percent of the American population, but they are largely absent from the technology-related fields. Even as the boom of the 1990s made technology one of the most desirable markets in business and education, African-Americans in 1995 earned just 1.8 percent of the Ph.D.'s conferred in computer science, 2.1 percent of the Ph.D.'s in engineering, 1.5 percent of them in the physical sciences and 0.6 percent of the Ph.D.'s in mathematics.

The U.S. Labor Department has cited and even fined several of the most prominent American hardware and software firms for discrimination. In fairness, many companies with a conspicuously low minority presence in their workforce say that the competition among them to recruit minorities is especially intense, and that there is just too small a pool of qualified candidates for them to meet their own minority staffing goals. The recruiters (and Randy spent years in this side of the business) say that this so-called digital-divide dilemma begins at home, with too few minority parents in tech careers to provide role models and networking resources; and in schools, where Black students were found to be significantly less likely than Whites to have access to the hardware and to be regular computer users. They want the minority candidates, but the candidates aren't there in sufficient quantity. So the problem snowballs.

R. Wayne Hicks, president of Black Data Processing Associates, says that when an African-American does defy the odds and carve a career in technology, there is an additional element of pressure that the average worker doesn't face. "The technology industry is perceived by many African-Americans as being more difficult to enter than many others," he says. "The cross that many African-American entrepreneurs need to bear is that they can't just be successful for themselves. They're representing the whole community, a whole culture. You'd like to think that he or she should be able to work without that extra pressure in the thought process, but if you're a successful African-American, you know you don't operate in a vacuum. Then again, it's a risk above and beyond the normal one, and that can be an inspiring challenge."

Which is how Randy Massengale looks at it.

"Like it or not," he says, "when you're Black in any profession, you're representing everyone, not just yourself. You're a role model. That's both a test and an opportunity. I knew early in my career that being African-American in this field meant having a high profile. My colleagues could do their jobs without that level of visibility I had. I didn't want to succeed or fail on any other basis than performance. It took me a while to understand how best to handle that, and my father's example helped me. I learned from him to treat the problem as the problem, not to treat myself as a victim of the problem. He got visible, tangible results in his landscaping business or in racing or in anything he did. You could see what he did—he could show you his work, and the more you knew about it, the better he looked to you. It wasn't a matter of guessing or spin or perception. There was proof. When I was young, the temptation was always there to take problems personally. I might have said, 'It's harder for me because I'm Black or because I'm young,' just as a woman might say, 'It's harder for me because I'm female,' or an Asian could say, 'It's harder because I'm Asian.' In some companies it's men over forty who feel put-upon for being older in areas where younger people are closer to the cutting edge. Name your demographic . . . problems happen to everyone. My dad couldn't tell people that his horse came in third because he's Black, or that he could do second-rate work on their yards because he grew up poor. And I learned to rely on what could be measured and proven, just as my dad did.

"I worked in corporate America a long time," he says. "And being raised by an entrepreneur, I was always looking for ways to exercise my potential as fully as I could. The technology business was the only area I saw that would test me from the standpoints of both intellectual and personal growth, and I liked it, but at every turn there seemed to be a limit on what I could do next. One company, for example—very well known, well respected, one of the Dow Jones Industrial Average companies . . . the way they're set up, they have 10 percent of the people on their staff doing the creative work, and the other 90 percent executing, and they're stuck with that. Throughout my corporate career I ran into that—it wasn't that I was unhappy at every turn, it's just that I felt underutilized. I felt I had the intellectual tools to create and the work ethic to execute. I called it the Five-and-Dime Theory. The Five-and-Dime Theory says that you may be able to do ten things, but they only hire you to do five. Even if the company is struggling with the other five, even if you have ideas that could help, they don't want the answer from you. That's very common in corporate settings, and very frustrating, and while it happens to everyone, particularly as an African-American I gravitate toward very difficult assignments to prove my worth. That always was good news. The bad news was, when I succeeded, they didn't want to promote me out of my position.

"I spent years with some of the best companies in my field, but I didn't get a chance to work in the hard-core technology sectors of those places. I still sit on the board of the Social Venture Partners here in Seattle—lots of former Microsoft people do that—funding new charitable ideas. I started a scholarship for minority students at my alma mater, Lewis & Clark College, where I sit on the board of trustees, and that's been very important to me and a real source of satisfaction. But those things can only take you so far. I feel that regardless of what I succeeded in doing so far, it's still incumbent on me to show what I can do.

"I really wanted to go head-to-head with other technologists. And you have to start somewhere, so I did. I'd been out of school for ten years, working, but I was constantly reading and journaling and studying. I went to my boss at Microsoft and told him I wanted to get a master's. He looked perplexed. 'Why would you go back to school?' he asked me. I had a great job; I was financially secure; I might have quit working entirely. But I didn't want to relax. I wanted a new challenge. I wanted to write and teach and stretch myself. I had to take my own vacation time and make extra commitments to get it done, but I had to make sure they understood how I felt—just like my father, I could not be stopped. I was going to get that degree.

"I wouldn't have had the courage to start this company if I hadn't done that. I finished in two years—when you have a goal and you've committed yourself to it, it's possible. My dad could commit to himself at a more visceral level than anyone else I ever knew. He doesn't care who tells him no—he's committed and he acts. If you tell him it can't be done, that doesn't affect his thinking. Tell him he can't be a disk jockey, tell him he can't own Thoroughbreds . . . it doesn't stop him. It was the same way for me going back to school.

"I remember doing a tree job with him and he was trying to show me what I was doing wrong and I said, 'Okay, I'm agreeing with you!'—he said, 'Yes, you're agreeing with me, but you're not *producing*.' I still think about that. It's one thing to agree with what's going on around you and even benefit from it, but I still have to produce myself. And it's been a labor of love for me. If he can wake up every morning and still go out and make it work, I can too. I got that persistence from watching him.

"The challenge Spinoza faces now is having the staying power to hang in there while it actually happens. We're at the front of the race. It's a challenging position to take. Plenty of the leaders in technology wait until someone else establishes a market for hardware or software and then they buy their way in after the road is opened. Many investors feel safer following the market that way. But I grew up as a risk taker, even a risk seeker, with my father's example to show me, and so I knew some of the emotional and intellectual obstacles that lay in this path. And that's the key challenge of building a business. It isn't just about managing your financial capital. It's mostly about managing your emotional capital, having the tenacity and the will to live with the stress and the risk, and handling that even when the doors don't open for you right away.

"My dad practiced that every day, literally knocking on doors one at a time.

"Working for him toughened my brothers and me to the real circumstances of the business world, and made us look for our own accountability when other people avoided facing their own. School doesn't give you that. I have guys here who got straight As, 1600s on the SATs, and I have to tell them sometimes the thing my dad used to say to us, 'Hey, man, walk like you're gonna take care of some *business*.' I mean, show some intent. Act like you want it. Don't get discouraged, don't slow down. Put yourself on the line. Academia doesn't teach that.

"And that's what makes a market—executing, day after day. It's one thing to have a five-year vision, but knowing what to do in the next five hours is where you succeed. My company used to be all by itself in this niche. Now we have competition. But we have the advantage because we executed every day. We wrote and tested hundreds of programs for our product. We built the relationships with the manufacturers that our competition doesn't have, and we have credibility in the field that they can't equal because we invested early, hung in and waited for the market to turn back up. And speaking of results, we're selling much more now than we were a year ago and we'll double that in the coming three months.

"There's no such thing as a perfect opportunity. There's always an excuse you can find not to move or make a decision, but hesitation doesn't get you anywhere. You couldn't hesitate if you worked with my father. We were taught early not to squander talent, and to make opportunities if we didn't see them. I want to lead in this, not to just take advantage of someone else's risk. I knew that this idea had a future regardless of the immediate state of the economy. Had I waited, the market would have happened without me. If I'd let it go by, I wouldn't be able to buy my way in, let alone develop my way in. After years of enduring some pretty adverse conditions, I think we're in a good position to be essential to the projector market, the home automation market and some emerging opportunities that were barely on anyone's radar when we started out. We're making fast progress in developing partnerships with equipment companies. When we started, we couldn't have gotten them to return phone calls. Now they're asking us to work with them."

NO MATTER how exciting it seems, many people in Randy's position would never have taken on the challenge. Any new company is vulnerable to a serious financial loss. Is the prospect of making more money the driving force? Randy laughs and indicates his nondescript office to answer that question.

"Money's overrated, to my mind," he says. "It can take away as much as it gives you. I don't care about it except for what it enables me to do for the world. It matters to me that I can endow a scholarship fund for minority students at Lewis & Clark, and that I can give my kids opportunities I want them to have. But having a lot . . . that never mattered.

"It's like this—my dad bought a Rolls-Royce. Man, that killed my interest in money right there. I was a senior in high school. I was sitting in this beautiful car, the best car you could get, and I thought, 'Hey, all this will do for me is get me from one place to another.' Drive in Los Angeles sometime. In the same crawling traffic jam on the 101 or the 405, you'll see hundred-thousand-dollar Ferraris and Bentleys moving five miles an hour behind beat-up pickup trucks and Toyotas. No one can get where they want to go faster because of the car they're in. Besides, in this field, the people who flaunt their wealth to work stick out like sore thumbs. Who could be impressed by some sports car when you're among multimillionaires every day? In the intellectual-capital business, it's what's between your ears that matters, not what you own. People in tech like the challenge of doing something hard and stretching themselves. They work for the love of that, not for another million dollars.

"My brothers and I were also shown that from those to whom much is given, much is required. We were blessed, very much so, by a great family and by good work. But our gifts and our blessings were there to be used. Dad used to quote Matthew 25, the parable of the talents. The man going on a journey gave his servants talents, five to one, two to another, one to the third. The first two invested and doubled the money, and the man was pleased and gave them additional responsibilities and opportunities to succeed. The third servant buried his master's money in the ground. He feared the risk, and he feared to use what he had. I look at it that way. If I was blessed with the means to set a good example, that's what I have to do. If it's hard, it's still what I have to do, and if I succeed, it might enable me to motivate someone else by example. That's what my brothers and I were taught: do the hard things, don't take any cheap success and don't ride someone else's wave."

Randy's course in the Albers School of Business and Economics at Seattle University has an unconventional reading list for a grad-level management class. Many of the models offered aren't from the business world at all. He calls it "the psychology of extraordinary performance," emphasizing personality traits, leadership styles and world history. Howard Gardner's *Leading Minds* and *Extraordinary Minds* and Chris Argyris's *Teaching Smart People How to Learn* are required texts. The additional recommended readings include books by social catalysts, people whose lives and work helped to change the world: *Days of Grace* by Arthur Ashe; *A Testament of Hope: The Essential Writings and Speeches of Martin Luther King, Jr.*; Blanche Wiesen Cook's two-volume biography of Eleanor Roosevelt; Gandhi's autobiography, *The Story of My Experiments with Truth*; Nelson Mandela's *Long Walk to Freedom*; and biographies of Jane Addams, Mao Tse-tung, Abraham Lincoln, George Marshall, Frederick Douglass, Barbara Jordan, Mozart and Pearl S. Buck. These people aren't just case studies for Randy. They're role models who changed things. He wants to do in his field, and in his life, something like what they accomplished in theirs, which is why he's working in a bare office instead of sailing on Puget Sound.

"I never heard of a really worthy role model, from Edison

to Gandhi to Mandela, who was satisfied hitting cruise control," Randy says. "There's such a thing as pride without merit; the pride you see in some big companies that comes with just getting in the door and wearing the logo shirt. It's not based on performance; it's just that you're part of the group. It smacks to me of being elitist, and it's too easy. I remember one of my old colleagues saying once that all you needed to do in some companies was go in, turn your computer on and hang your jacket over the back of the chair. You could vanish for hours! People would think you were out to a meeting or something. He was only half joking. In some big companies you can bury yourself in the organizational chart, enjoy a prestigious title and a steady check and have hardly any direct responsibility. That's not me.

"My dad was accountable for everything he did all his life—he took pride in the hard things, not in the easy ones. I never forgot that lesson. That's how we work here. That's why we're going to succeed."

Randy's course grew out of his own experience: in 2004 he was one of twenty-five winners in a national essay contest commemorating the twenty-fifth anniversary of the cable news network C-SPAN. Randy's essay described how C-SPAN's literary program Booknotes motivated him in 1997 to form an executive-mentorship program at Microsoft for the company's young African-American men. The program still exists, and many of its members have been promoted within Microsoft or have gone on to leadership at other companies. That mentoring program gave him the framework for Extraordinary Leaders. "I have two passions," he told C-SPAN. "Developing technology and developing people." Randy and his wife, Kit, do the latter by supporting minority students at Lewis & Clark, where Randy and Kit met as students. After Randy leaves Spinoza for the day, he and Kit gather some local L&C alumni at a Seattle restaurant to meet the college's new president, to reunite with Randy's faculty mentor and to congratulate the recipient of the Randy Massengale Scholarship, a $10,000, two-year scholarship awarded annually to a sophomore of African-American, Native-American, Hispanic-American or Asian-American descent for use in the student's junior and senior years. Academic performance is one of the requirements for the award, but equally important is that the applicants have a history of community service. Along with The Cherubs, a Seattle venture capital group Randy founded, his work with Social Venture Partners, and the Massengale Family Foundation, which Kit runs in support of education and children's causes, Randy's involvement as a trustee at Lewis & Clark is a way he can give something back.

At the top of the list of things Randy seeks to build are himself and his family. He and Kit have three children. They set the bar high. "Every New Year's, my family talks together about what we want from ourselves, what we want to accomplish in the coming year, and we try to manage our lives to that theme. A Year of Giving, for example . . . that year we looked at how to give, how to commit ourselves to a cause or an organization. We asked when should you give, what was our philanthropic philosophy, who benefits? A Year of Leadership: we all look for ways to take on positions of responsibility. The kids can find ways to do this even when they're little; something as simple as saving spare change in a jar and regularly emptying that jar for some local cause got them thinking about the idea and executing on it. They got into FareStart, an organization in Seattle that provides meals to people and trains people to work in the food service industry. Through Social Venture Partners, my kids meet kids who might be homeless, and get involved in fundraisers to plan charitable investments. My Year of Education was when I decided to go back to school and get my advanced degree. When I was full time in grad school I still read two additional books a month. I was pushing myself to learn. Last year we set ourselves to the Year of Coming Out, meaning taking a higher public profile on things like C-SPAN. I'd never have done that before. I felt it was time to get involved in more media-related things and issues, talking to the press more and taking more responsibility in the community. I was looking for more ways to be accountable. And it sent a signal to my kids. There's a tendency I see sometimes in African-American families to put intellectual performance second or even to dismiss it as not important compared with athletic ability. My son's a good athlete, but I wasn't going to let anyone, including him, categorize him based on the fact that he's gifted on the basketball court. Coming aboveground and taking a high profile in intellectual challenges showed my kids and this community that my family values intellectual development. My kids' teachers know that a lot is expected of my children. They're accountable, like I am, and they'll shoulder that as an opportunity to distinguish themselves. So we're all stretching ourselves to be more and to do more. And that makes our lives rich.

"None of us in my family is threatened by new opportunities and situations. We're not happy unless we're confronting the challenges of building and growing. We look for them. We look for criticism to make us sharper and stronger; we let our mistakes become material for growing. We persist because that's the point. And that's the reward."

LESSON FIVE

FEARLESSNESS

Preface by Fred D. Gray, Esq.

The luxury of history is to look back on a time and detect in it a "movement," a change that may have taken decades to achieve and may have shifted the destiny of a nation. This is particularly true of the Montgomery, Alabama, Bus Boycott and the role I played in, as history now calls it, the beginning of the Civil Rights Movement. Such retrospection tempts us to give a label to such a time, and to study it as a story, with a beginning, a middle and an end, as though the story is done, even when it is not. In relegating them to history, we might be tempted to treat the trials and hardships of such times as curiosities of the past, but in fact they are bridges for building the future.

Students today can reflect on the time when Americans, and particularly African-Americans, strove to create a land free of the evils of racism and segregation, cleansed of hypocrisy that promised "equal justice under law" to all, while systematically betraying that promise to many. Even with the best intentions, and with due respect for those of us who sacrificed greatly during those years, many Americans today are lulled into thinking that because we call that time the "Civil Rights Era" and we had some successes, that the story is over, and that we, as one nation at last, have moved on. The story is not over. There is no such place as a "level playing field" in America. The struggle continues.

Living a story is very different from reflecting upon it.

Stories have an inexorable momentum forward. Life does not. What seems to history to have been inevitable was in truth a matter of individual actions and personal decisions made in the hard light of real danger, taking into account not just overall goals and ideals, but personal risks and sacrifices. Making change happen is hard work. There are obstacles of time and lack of resources. There are adversaries, and even enemies. There are losses to be borne. There are days, even years, when the course of history seems to flow not forward toward any ideal day, but backward toward inequality. That was true during the Civil Rights Era. It will be true again for those of you who seek to make your world better.

It took fearlessness to create successful change during the Civil Rights Movement. Fearlessness will be needed again by anyone who seeks to build a better world, or more simply a meaningful life and a good family. This lesson of the past must not be just remembered. You must live fearlessness. You must make it your own.

Fred D. Gray is one of the nation's preeminent civil rights attorneys. He helped make history when he represented Rosa Parks and was counsel for Dr. Martin Luther King, Jr. He represented the Freedom Riders, the Selma-to-Montgomery marchers, the victims of the Tuskegee Syphilis Study, and many more seeking equality and justice. In 2004, he received the Thurgood Marshall Award from the American Bar Association.

BIDDY MASON PARK is a little courtyard off Spring Street between Third and Fourth in downtown Los Angeles, across from the Ronald Reagan Building, in the midst of some of the most valuable real estate in the United States. Born in the South in 1818, Bridget "Biddy" Mason was the property of Robert Marion Smith, who is thought to have fathered Biddy's three daughters. In 1847, Smith converted to Mormonism and moved his household to the Utah Territory. Biddy herded the cattle, tended the children, midwifed for others in the caravan and cooked along the two-thousand-mile trek.

Smith moved again in 1851 to a Mormon community in San Bernardino, east of what today is Los Angeles. Like many others who moved with their human property to California, Smith seems not to have known that it was officially free. The California constitution of 1849 stated explicitly that "neither slavery nor involuntary servitude shall ever be tolerated in this state."

Smith resolved to take his slaves to Texas. Biddy Mason refused to go. She sued for her freedom, and in 1856 a judge ruled that she and her daughters were "entitled to their freedom and are free forever." A copy of the ruling is set into the wall of the park named for her.

So began one of the city's most remarkable business careers. Biddy Mason invested wisely in residential and commercial real estate around this neighborhood, including a modest house at 331 Spring Street where she lived from 1866 to 1891 on land she bought for $250. Biddy's home was called "The House of the Open Hand" because she spent freely to feed and clothe the needy through times of flood and drought. "If you hold your hand closed," she said, "nothing good can come in. The open hand is blessed, for it gives in abundance, even as it receives." As Los Angeles grew, so did Biddy's fortune. She founded First African Methodist Episcopal Church, the city's first Black church. She educated her children and grandchildren. One of her grandsons, Robert, was successful in politics and business and became one of the wealthiest African-Americans in Los Angeles.

By the time she died in 1891, the slave girl who walked to California had left a fortune of $300,000. The city knew her as "Auntie Mason" and "Grandma Mason." In 1998 a marker was finally placed on her grave in Boyle Heights, and Los Angeles dedicated this memorial to her near where The House of the Open Hand once stood.

IN 1965, Joe Massengale had left his radio career to concentrate on his thriving tree-trimming and landscaping business. Joe and his brothers still worked together on many jobs, often bringing their sons along. He was living in a new home in the integrated neighborhood called View Park. Joe's five sons, now including one-year-old Patrick, lived not far away with their mother Dorothy, Joe's first wife, and spent weekends and summers helping their father.

The early Civil Rights Era in Los Angeles was relatively peaceful compared with the East Coast cities where violence broke out in the summer of 1964. Harlem, Rochester, Chicago, Jersey City, Paterson, Elizabeth and Philadelphia all suffered rioting as unrest in their African-American communities exploded into violence. Los Angeles's larger size might have eased the pressure for a while, but the population of Joe's old neighborhood multiplied rapidly as the migration from the South continued. Pleasant integrated areas like View Park where Blacks were welcome to buy were rare. California voters sought to block the fair-housing provisions of the 1965 Civil Rights Act by passing their own state proposition circumventing the national law and effectively extending segregationist housing sale and rental practices in the state. The Supreme Court reversed the proposition, but the intent lingered.

Meanwhile, in the established Black neighborhoods, there were fewer jobs and fewer easier options for getting in and out to work as the old Red Car light rail lines were torn up and replaced with buses. Broken homes, unemployment and deteriorating properties were the norm as South Central weakened.

The anger built. A few days before Biddy Mason's 147th birthday, Los Angeles caught fire.

AT AROUND seven on the hot evening of August 11, 1965, a California Highway Patrol officer made a routine traffic stop of a suspected drunk driver in South Central. The arrest turned into a scuffle, and a crowd gathered. More officers were called to the scene. More people gathered to protest. It was a fuse waiting for a spark. Dozens of people turned to hundreds, shouting, angry. A rock or a bottle flew and fighting broke out. By midnight there were nineteen injured police officers, nearly three dozen arrests and fifty vehicles damaged. People hoped it might be over. On the twelfth, community leaders met and tried to quell tempers, but meanwhile, gangs mobilized and stockpiled Molotov cocktails. When night fell, Watts was engulfed in flames, with thousand of people rioting, burning and looting.

The riot hit home for Joe Massengale and his family. Joe's sons were young, but 450 boys and over 70 girls were arrested in the conflict, so youth offered no safe harbor.

Michael Massengale was eleven years old. "I remember how heated it was," he says. "Watts back then was violence ready to happen. There was a different climate inside the LAPD. You didn't even look at a policeman if you were Black in Los Angeles because you'd get pulled over. My father got arrested all the time when he was working. It was almost permissible that you'd get pulled out of the car and beaten during the [Mayor Sam] Yorty–[Police Chief William H.] Parker days; they were practically White supremacists.

"I was just a kid. I was more interested in baseball than in the Black Power Movement. I didn't know much about Dr. King or Malcolm X. We lived on 80th Street with our mother. That was a mixed neighborhood, but when we first moved there in 1957, someone burned a cross on our lawn. We were close to the area of the rioting as it came down Vermont Avenue. There were military vehicles in the street. My mother wouldn't let us go out. Some guys came by our house and knocked on the door and tried to get us to take part, but my father called us and told us to stay inside. We watched it on TV. We knew that neighborhood where it was happening; we used to go shopping there for groceries and clothes, and we always drove through during the holidays to see the Christmas decorations because there was such pride of ownership there. Imagine watching all that being destroyed."

Two of Joe's nephews were a little older, and they engaged themselves directly. Charles and Oliver Massengale, sons of Joe's older brother Oliver, often worked with Joe and his boys on big jobs. They were already deeply involved in the Black Power movement as members of the closest circle around Dr. Maulana Karenga, who shortly after the riots founded Organization US. Groups that disparaged US insisted that "US" stood for United Slaves; in fact it meant simply Black people, "us" and not "them."

The organization sought to revive Afrocentric culture and pride and ultimately to create a separate community. US was less militant than some of its counterparts such as the Black Panthers, more in line with the nineteenth-century Black nationalists such as Marcus Garvey, and Malcolm X in the twentieth. The members wore African clothes and hairstyles, adopted Swahili names and invented a new Afrocentric holiday, Kwanzaa. Charles and Oliver were present at the first one in a South Central apartment.

US members took an oath of loyalty to the organization

and its founder. They followed strict rules about their personal conduct and participation. The short-term goal was creating a new Black culture emphasizing pride and African heritage, around a quasi-religious spirituality built on native African beliefs. Its long-term goals were more ominous: intellectual and ideological separation, and possibly even guerrilla war.

Charles and Oliver Massengale took new names, Sigidi and Heshimu. Sigidi was a praise name of Zulu origin; Heshimu meant "honor and respect" in Swahili.

Oliver Massengale Heshimu today still lives in South Central in a house decorated with his collection of African art. "I'd been in the Air Force from '62 to '64," he says, "and I had some bad experiences with racism—incidents of a kind I'd never encountered in my life. I was appalled, and I was angry. I revolted to the point of getting court-martialed and discharged. My brother Charles, the same. He was at Grambling in Louisiana, and he saw racism like he'd never seen. He started sending me recordings of Malcolm X. I'd never heard of the man; he'd just been killed and I'd never known who he was. We listened carefully to everything we heard. By the time the revolt in Watts happened, we both had all this energy and no place to put it.

"We started hearing of Ron Karenga, 'Maulana' as he was called, Swahili for 'master teacher.' He was conducing Swahili classes at Fremont High School for adults, and we started going. Before this I viewed Africa as a good place to be away from. I had no idea of my heritage. I had no idea that in ancient times there were Black kings, Black queens, Black conquerors, Black scholars, Black doctors. That's what we started learning, and we started attending meetings on Black nationalist culture at a little bookstore. US hadn't even been formed yet. My brother and I sat in on the initial planning and study group called the Circle of Seven. From those meetings, US grew.

"When the revolt in Watts broke out, my brother Charles was working in the landscaping business with our uncle Joe, and there were disagreements in the family about all of this. Joe believed it wasn't about Black versus White; he just wanted to be successful. Color didn't really matter to him. He hardly talked about it. He was against violence. He was against destruction. He was always positive, always building. I never saw him tear down anything. Joe stayed focused and steadfast to his purpose. I was angry. I was out in the street fighting. I think Joe felt the same sense of pain and suffering as the rest of us did. But he felt that economics was the way out of that. I didn't. A lot of us in the Movement didn't. We felt that equality and justice needed attention."

Young men from US were featured in a military-style drill on the cover of *Life* in July 1966. By 1967, it was active throughout the city, and its members were working with sympathetic networks all over the country. US even had members among the American servicemen in Vietnam. As the organization evolved into a hierarchy, Oliver Heshimu was a *Mwalimu*, a teacher. "I was one of the seven teachers in the group, and we went all over the country talking about Black Nationalism. We were trying to build a Black Congress of organizations based in Los Angeles. The authorities tried any way they could to prevent us from assembling. As we started becoming more popular in the neighborhood we'd speak at high schools and to the gangs, and the more we showed we could have a positive influence, the more the authorities tried saying we were on the campus illegally or busting us. We were raided constantly. The doors were kicked in; there was the serious possibility of being killed. We were being attacked by the FBI. It's all documented. They viewed us as subversives and feared the power we had in the community. Our objective was to change the minds of our people, and heighten their consciousness. We met with resistance from the local police; the LAPD started flying helicopters over the city 24/7, and our apartments would get lit up. When the revolt broke out in Watts, we were in the street going toe to toe."

Soon, Heshimu oversaw the *Simba Wachanga*, the Young Lions—US's paramilitary wing. They trained intensively in ideology, martial arts and weapons, and took an oath including the words "We must believe in our cause and be willing to die for it . . . and stop pretending revolution and make it." This was not an idle promise. A photo in Heshimu's study shows him carrying shotguns and pistols on a South Central street. Not only were Heshimu and his brother fighting the authorities, but US was also at direct odds with other Black activists, particularly the Black Panthers. A shootout in 1969 between US and the Panthers left two men dead.

No issue ever divided Joe Massengale's family the way this conflict did. Joe remained on good terms with his nephews, but he was adamant about where he and his sons stood. "I was always on my nephews about that—'Man,' I told them, 'what you're talking about is *nothing*.

" 'It's going to get you in a lot of trouble,' I told them. They said, 'You just want to stay up on top of the hill there in View Park; you don't want to be around Black folks,' something like that . . . it got intense sometimes. The differences over an issue like this even inside a family can be extreme. I respected them, and I still do, but if one of my sons had gotten involved I'd have objected very strongly. I never spoke against America. I wouldn't do it. I was old enough to know that even when there were racial differences here, things were still better here than it was in other places. Things in my family were cordial and my nephews and I always talked, but no, I didn't go for what they were doing."

Joe was not fully aware of how his sons felt. Larry, his third, remembers, "From the time I was thirteen, up to maybe seventeen, during the time Heshimu and Sigidi were with US, I related to how they felt. My friends and I were done with the idea of civil disobedience and nonviolent protest. We were sick of it. We wanted justice and we were going to take it if we had to. We were going to get in people's faces. I was more militant than my father understood. I didn't let him see it, knowing how he felt, but I attended Black Panther Party rallies and meetings. My friends and I used the Black Power salute, wore the black jackets and the berets. My cousins were on the educational vanguard of the Movement. The Panthers were more militant, advocates of the "by any means necessary" philosophy of Malcolm X. Some of my teachers in school had that famous picture of Huey P. Newton in the rattan chair, with the spear and the shotgun, on the wall. I read Newton and Cleaver and Che Guevera; I read Mao, *The Little Red Book*, in the tenth grade. I don't think my father ever realized how much it affected me. He never saw me wearing the beret. I wouldn't have done that in front of him. I wanted confrontation. My dad's way with that was never to indulge in confrontation for confrontation's sake. He had it in him, certainly, but he kept his temper in check. He had his priorities."

Randy agrees. "People have natural preferences for things that are like them, and that's fine as long as you're aware of it and not trapped by it. Decisions that you make, how you spend your time . . . once you lock in to a way, and say that is the only way to think, that's a form of bigotry that calcifies your mind and your spirit. Our dad would expose us to all different types of people, on the job, in our home, in different kinds of churches, so that we never looked at race as a determining factor about a person. If he saw that a Black man did a White man wrong, he was all over that guy. That wasn't the case with many people. I knew Black men who came out of the South, who might have been coaches in school or people my dad worked with, who almost gave you license to hate White people because of what they'd gone through themselves. It's easy to understand; having grown up with the adversity they faced, they felt they needed to think with the same weapons that had been used against them. But my dad didn't fall into that trap. He said, 'Listen, I have some baggage myself, but that's not yours, and it doesn't belong to the kids you associate with. You guys go out there and pick whoever you think is right for you to be your friends based on their character.'

"He was as good as his word," Randy recalls. "I was dating a White girl when I was in high school. Her father was upset about it. She and I talked to my dad and he said, 'Well, we have a lot of problems in this house, but racism isn't one of them.'"

"I don't go for any idea of racial identity or 'staying on

your side of town,' Joe says. "My side of town is *America*. I get along with anyone who wants to get along with me. I wasn't going to listen to anything different. I never had any trouble where I lived. View Park was peaceful. We always got along with the neighbors there; people shared meals and my kids had friends there and everyone was gracious. I wasn't looking to make some kind of political statement by moving there, I just wanted a nice house. And I didn't change churches and didn't change my friends just because of where I lived.

"It's easy to understand how some people might have been attracted to the Movement, especially young people, I guess, but that was some bad stuff . . . and my nephews Charles and Oliver almost got killed for it. Someone bombed the apartment where they were staying. My boys weren't too young to get seriously involved. A lot of the kids who got into US were teenagers, so my sons were vulnerable. We talked about it. I think they respected my experience and my way of seeing things. They might have gotten into trouble the way kids do but they never did any real damage, and we worked hard together. I never went to any of the Movement meetings. I was in the church I wanted to be in and doing what I wanted to be doing, and nothing was going to change that. I knew who I was; I didn't question myself. I never told my sons to stay away from it; they just knew to do what was right, and they didn't feel that that was right. And after all that fighting, all that destruction, people who did it still had to come back into the world and ask for a job."

US numbered just a few hundred people at its height, but thousands were of the same mindset as Watts burned. By Biddy Mason's birthday in 1965, 150 square blocks of Los

Angeles was a war zone. The National Guard rolled down Central Avenue in tanks. Fifty-caliber machine guns sat ready on corners as ten thousand uniformed troops carried rifles in the streets.

Fuel for the fires came from an innocent slogan used by one of Joe Massengale's colleagues in radio. Joe's place among the leading Black disk jockeys was taken by Nathaniel "Magnificent" Montague, a charismatic journeyman whose show, in contrast to Joe's low-key style, was, he said, "a fire-and-brimstone church service in which I was the Lord, R&B music was the Old Testament, and the kids were the disciples." Montague's signature line had been used by him in New York and Chicago to get his audience energized, but in Los Angeles, it turned from a declaration about hot music into a battle cry for the rioting: *Burn, baby! Burn!*" Montague was appalled to hear it being used to mobilize the looters, and switched to "Have mercy!"

By the last day, August 16, the toll was devastating. Over thirty-five thousand people were thought to have rioted, with tens of thousands more watching. Thirty-four were dead, over a thousand were injured and four thousand were arrested. Property damage was estimated at over $200 million. It was heartbreaking and frightening for the nation to watch.

"Of course there was anger. There were grievances. People suffered," Joe says. "I suffered too, in Marshall and in Los Angeles. But there's no such thing as getting even. Burning down a business, Black or White—how is that getting even? And what good is getting even? I wanted to do better than just get even. I wanted to exceed what people expected of me, and I wanted that for my sons. Getting even only makes you weaker.

Deuteronomy 32:35: 'To me belongeth vengeance and recompense . . .' That's not what we do in my family. It only leads to more killing.

"There are wars going on here in Los Angeles right now that started twenty years ago. These young men . . . one loses a friend and takes his revenge, then the other side takes theirs . . . it only leads to more pain and bloodshed, and no one's life is any better for that. I took the bad things that happened to me as incentive to grow, not as a reason to get back at someone. So much of the vengeance that was taken ultimately just damaged the people who took it. It wasn't a victory for anyone, not in 1965 and not when people rioted again in 1992. It was just a waste. The damage was done, and this city still hasn't recovered. I like progress, and that's not it. I tried to do something positive instead. I didn't permit myself to get angry.

"An angry man does foolish things. A man who goes door to door the way I did has to make himself adaptable. You need resilience. You can't get angry at failure or setbacks. I always got a lot more feeling of satisfaction out of the good encounters I had, the friendly people, the kind ones, than I ever did out of the confrontations, and at the end when I look back those are the ones I treasure . . . people whose respect I earned, people who earned mine. The good people I met all showed me what happens when you treat people like you want to be treated yourself. If my mortgage needs to be paid, am I going to sit here or am I going to get out there and hustle? Are you going to do what you do worst, and make everything worse, or do what you do best and get back on your feet?

"I can't buy the idea that someone isn't 'treated well'—

what's that mean, 'treated'? I think you can compound your problems fast if you wait for people to 'treat' you. You do good things first and put the best feeling out there and you'll get that back. I don't ask people to treat me well—I give respect first. It doesn't cost anything to be nice, and I'm not about to sacrifice that feeling because in the end that's all that comes back. You give good feelings and you get them back all the time.

"I wasn't afraid to be exactly who I was," Joe says. "I had a sense of my own independence, my own identity, at a time when people wanted to classify themselves on one side or another of an issue. People are people and I wasn't going to be anyone else's label. That's just another way of being fearful. I wasn't afraid to be who I was and to take people for who they were. That's one side of fearlessness. Another side is prudence and caution. People with no fear and no caution get into trouble—fearlessness doesn't mean being reckless. I'm always cautious about that one moment of recklessness that I'll have to pay for the rest of my life. I fear the cost of saying something hurtful that I'll never have a chance to take back.

"I think of my dad back in Marshall when moments of fear come up. Two guys who cut logs for him got to drinking and got in a fight one Saturday evening. My dad didn't go away. They threw some punches, and one of them jumped on the other guy, beat him down and punched him in the face. My dad broke it up and told them, just stop it. But the guy who was down picked up a brick. He pulled back to throw it, and my dad walked up, just walked up and said, 'Don't you hit that man. Don't you do it.' The man says, 'Mister Hugh, if you don't get out of the way I'm going to hit *you*.' My dad said,

'No . . . you're going to put that brick down.' The man just put the brick down. I can still see that. That's the kind of guy he was. Walked a straight and narrow line all the time. Treated everybody right and didn't take very much. Humble man, but he didn't bend.

"So I tried to do my best to govern that anger in me and share only the best part of myself. The most important thing I did for my sons was just to talk. I just talked straight about conduct and behavior and character as we went out doing our jobs. To me it was common sense, and every parent's supposed to have some of that to share with kids. My experience showed me things they needed to understand, and I tried to pass that along. It was common sense. Controlling your destiny doesn't mean burning down a building. It means educating yourself, getting a position in life and doing something positive for where you live."

AT THE height of Joe's success in racing, he fulfilled a dream by buying a ranch in Fallbrook, about a hundred miles south of Los Angeles, close to one of the most beautiful tracks in the country, the Del Mar Thoroughbred Club.

It was the perfect place for a horseman. His second marriage had ended, and Joe hoped to make a fresh start and succeed as a full-time Thoroughbred boarder and breeder. The move itself was an act of fearlessness: Fallbrook was the base for the White Aryan Resistance, a notoriously racist organization run by a former Grand Master of the Ku Klux Klan. The organization's Web site still offers "racist games" and "racist cartoons," and sells White supremacist merchandise, Nazi jewelry, videos and books from a Fallbrook PO box.

"I wanted to get away from Los Angeles," Joe says. "I was just divorced and looking to start over; I was loving the racing game and looking to get better at it. I liked everything about owning horses, and I was willing to do anything I could to learn from the people who knew more than I knew. Not just owners, but trainers, riders, anybody who had knowledge to share. I wanted to know the job just like I knew the tree business, hands-on. There wasn't anything I wasn't willing to do; if I could learn by watching someone nail on a shoe, I did it. And the place was beautiful, very much like Marshall. I was used to small-town living. Camp Pendleton was literally next door. The fence ran about fifty feet from my front door. Everyone knew everyone else, people watched you and how you behaved. A good reputation was your most valuable possession. It was my kind of place."

The Rolling JM Ranch was ten acres set in a green bowl in the hills with a cream-colored bungalow, grassy pastures and palm trees. Joe built a brick patio, rebuilt the barns and paddocks and settled in for what he hoped would be a long career. He was the only African-American homeowner there, and one of just a handful of Blacks in the town. There were minor harassments from the local police, but generally he found people friendly and felt welcome. He even opened a little restaurant to indulge in another hobby, cooking. "Joe's Oak Pit Bar-B-Que," Joe says with a smile. "We started on a Friday afternoon and, man, you couldn't get near it. I don't know anyone who doesn't love good barbecue. We had lines out the door every night. I did radio spots on Fridays on the local radio station. The Marines from Pendleton practically lived there."

Surprisingly, there was no trouble at all with the supremacists. "Nothing related to the Klan ever happened, though their leader lived next ranch over," he remembers. "One night my dogs got loose and killed one of his sheep. He sent some-one over and I apologized, wrote a check for the damage, and that was it. There wasn't any trouble. It was my fault. I took responsibility and I paid for it. There wasn't any confrontation about it because no one looked at it as a racial issue or any-thing like that. I'd have talked with the man himself, anytime. He was like any other neighbor as far as I was concerned, and from my side at least we'd have gotten along. I know a man will say a lot of things on the radio that he wouldn't say at his front door. On the other hand, if he provoked something, just to do it, I wouldn't have let that stand. I wasn't going to look for trouble but I wasn't about to take any.

"Funny thing—turns out White supremacists like barbe-cue like anyone else. I saw them in my restaurant all the time. Understand, I'm not a violent man, not an angry man, but I'd never let someone hurt me or my family. But you have to know what's going on around you. That time with my father and the mules, back in Marshall . . . he was right to be angry about the neighbor who wanted three or four dollars every time our mules got out. But Dad should have built better fences, too. If he'd gone up to that man's place with a rifle, well, that would have been suicide. What did it matter if he was right or wrong if he left a widow and thirteen kids?

"Of course it wasn't fair the way the police talked to me when I was a kid shining shoes on the street for a nickel: 'You niggers get back, you got no business here,' and they'd hit me with a billy club; sure, I thought about that kind of thing and I still feel angry sometimes. But when you become a man you have to let that anger go—*you cannot make progress just being angry.* I am not mad with anyone about what happened to me. I want my sons to understand it because all that happened and all I felt about it helped to make who I am, but I don't want to carry anger with me. I wasn't a victim. I'm not going to feel like a victim.

"My nephews made their choice and I made mine. I think some people felt they had no choice but to fight, and they stayed angry to do it. I never did because I had something else in mind. It's always a choice. I wasn't going to throw my future away and my sons' futures away, on a moment of fear and anger that I couldn't get back.

"I just believe that with all the people I've met, all the people I've worked for, I never felt like an underdog. It might have looked that way, me being a landscaper working for professionals and wealthy folks, but I never felt intimidated and I never felt inferior. That's where anger comes from. I never felt that.

"Racial prejudice is holy hell. I'd seen enough of it. So I made friends in Fallbrook. I got along with people and enjoyed the life."

Heaven in Fallbrook lasted ten years.

"It was a dream home," Joe says. "Such a beautiful place. But I was in over my head trying to be a breeder. You can't keep a ranch like that on what your horses win. I went at it the wrong way, hoping to live on winnings, and the cash flow wasn't enough. Fearlessness isn't a good idea if you don't know what you're doing. You go into something not paying attention, you're in serious trouble. I found that out by training horses—you can feed a Thoroughbred, rub him down, walk him down in the pasture and he'll be playing with you, nuzzling your back, and the next second he'll kill you. That's the mustang in them. You'd better have a healthy sense of awareness about that. It's the same way with any business and any financial obligation you take in. In the end the ranch didn't pay for itself. I couldn't sustain it on racing purses and breeding money. I had to sell. I ended up giving most of the horses away."

He was down to the change in his pockets. At sixty, he went back to work. Joe moved back to Los Angeles and moved in with Michael. He called his old clients and restarted the tree business.

"I left Fallbrook with all my debts paid. I'd gotten loans against my cars and personal things, but when I left, I was clear. I had four hundred dollars and I was starting over. And man—I felt peace of mind. I wasn't afraid of anything. My mind was clear, and when your mind is clear, you've got a shot. I just wanted to get to work.

"There's broke and there's poor," Joe says. "Being broke is where you are today. Being poor is a mentality. Money isn't going to help you if you're poor in your heart, in your spirit. I had direction. I had goals. I knew I'd be back."

Ahead lay not only the challenge of starting over in business, but the greatest test Joe would face as a father.

There are men out there who can shun responsibility. They won't take the chances to learn about life, put their own interests second, and build. I was taught different—you make your bed, you lie in it. My wife tells me I'm always preaching about "doing the right thing," but I say, Hey, you're my girl, and Lena's my child, and I'm responsible, bottom line. That's making me a better man to embrace that.

IF HER father has anything to say about it, Lena Payton Massengale will be a scholar-athlete by the time she makes it to preschool. She tends to shun dolls and plush toys in favor of books and basketballs, including the regulation ones that come up to her waist. At eighteen months old, she has two toy backboards, and she delights in delighting her father, who can be a pretty rigorous coach. The kid can take it to the hole.

When Lena was born, Patrick wrote his brothers.

Dear Brothers,

    I apologize for not writing sooner. I have been on the go, and when I have a minute, I try to get some rest. In the meantime I'm working on some home runs, if you know what I mean. When you don't have a job and you try to create your own, the critics might try and disrupt your progress. The difference between us and the critics is that they can be silenced. Ambition never rests.

I am now sitting down to write and to thank you for your support. Without my family, not only would I be nothing, it would be worse. I would be normal.

Recently Gigi and I have been blessed with the birth of Lena Payton Massengale. Wow . . . I am still in shock. We are blessed. The most important thing when you go through this deal is that the kid comes into the world healthy. That was my only concern, not, do I have enough money to take care of this child? Or, will I not be a fit parent because of lack of experience? And by the grace of God, we won. Lena Payton Massengale came out as healthy as an ox. Mean as a pit bull.

I stayed on my knees praying every day that this kid would not be hurt by anything I did in my past. I prayed that she would enter the world as an example of God's love. I also prayed that God would send her into the world kicking and screaming, mean and tough. The Lord put some extra efforts into creating these traits in Lena's personality. The end result is that we have been blessed with Lena's presence, and I cannot take credit for any of that. I thank God, Gigi and you.

Every effort made on this kid's behalf is worth it. As you know, I don't drive in snow, so one of the cool things that I enjoy doing is walking to the store three-fourths of a mile in 8 degrees with a wind-chill of –4 to get formula and firewood for my little girl. People look at me like I am crazy, but the store managers and employees say, "Pat-man, Lena's out of formula again?" And proceed to give me extra cans of formula or offer me a ride home.

Man, that's love, and love still prevails.

Again fellas, thank you for your support. Thank you so much. I love you so much. Much love to your families, and please kiss them for us. Lena has and will continue to have a very blessed life because of God and you.

Love, Uncle P.

Lena is named for Lena Calhoun Horne, whom her grandfather Joe Massengale saw at the Club Alabam in South Central Los Angeles back in the 1940s. Born in Brooklyn, Lena Horne slept on tour buses when she was declined a room at the hotels where she sang. A favorite in World War II, she refused to perform before audiences of segregated troops, or to groups where German prisoners-of-war were seated in front of African-American GI's. She survived the blacklists of the 1950s and was recognized as a Kennedy Center Honoree in 1984. "You have to be taught to be second class," she said once. "You're not born that way."

Lena Massengale's other namesake comes from a different pursuit, but from the same spirit. Walter Payton, forever known as "Sweetness" to Chicago football fans, is third on the NFL's all-time rushing list. Small for his size, Payton was known for tenacity and durability on the gridiron, and for grace and dignity off it. He died too young. "I want to be remembered as the guy who gave his all whenever he was on the field," he said. He is.

Patrick admires Lena Horne for her beauty and sophistication, and loves Walter Payton for his resiliency and dignity. "I hope those names will signify strength and class for my daughter," Pat says as Lena plays. "She's a tough customer herself.

Her second day in the world, about midnight, the nurse came in and took her to the nursery so my wife could get a little rest. Thirty minutes later I heard screaming and yelling like the place was being taken apart. The nurse brought Lena back and said, 'There's nothing we can do for this kid, she's being too ornery.' That's when I was sure she was my daughter."

PATRICK AND his wife run Air-All Dynamics, mobile cleaning for aircraft and commercial vehicles, and Big Pat's BBQ Express, a catering company, in the Denver area. Trucks and trailers for both businesses are parked outside as Lena plays. Pat was out last night cooking until three A.M.

"When you ask me what my father has meant to me over the years," he says, "it's important to know that my parents were separated before I was born, and divorced when I was five. I was the fifth of their sons. I lived with my father only two years. What I learned from him, I learned working with him and visiting, and I got a great deal of him from my brothers.

"I left home pretty early, at seventeen. I wasn't doing well in school in Los Angeles, and I went to Oregon where Joe Jr. and Randy had studied, to a community college. I stayed a year and a half or so, and then I wanted to go out on my own.

"I did a little homework and narrowed the list to three places, Denver, Houston and Chicago. Coming to Denver was almost a matter of tossing a dart at a board. That was twenty years ago. I didn't know a soul. I got off the plane with a footlocker of clothes and a little black-and-white TV.

"I was looking for something, but I wasn't sure what. I wanted to get involved in financial services, or maybe the oil business. I landed a job interview with a financial planning company, hoping to become a broker's assistant. The branch manager tore me to shreds. 'You have no education,' he said. 'What makes you think you can come to work in this office?' I walked out of there just sweating. The young White dude waiting for his interview saw me come out and he said, 'Man, what happened? You're in bad shape.'" Pat laughs. "The guy tore up his application there and then. He walked out with me. We're still friends.

"I just scuffled for a while here in Denver, but I'd watched my dad and my brothers fall and keep going. They know how to perform when the chips are down. Now, almost twenty years later, my wife and I have a couple of small businesses. Like any people building something, we've seen good times and tough times. But we're still here. If you ask me for one lesson my dad taught me that I use today in my work and my life, it's fearlessness.

"It's not a sometime thing. Fear is looking for you. It'll show up in ways you don't expect. You make compromises with it, and you don't even realize it's happening. So you have to watch for it. You have to keep it away."

"I've seen my dad at moments when trouble broke out. You know how it is, it's either fight or flight—well, I never saw him retreat or run; never saw him stand back in the face of danger, and I mean physical danger. He was very protective of his family and his children. He'd never let anyone take advantage physically of us or his crew or someone else.

"Some of the impressions I have are very vivid. Once when

I was in the fourth or fifth grade, there was trouble in the neighborhood. Some guy on the street was acting crazy. There was no way to know if he had a gun. He could have, easily— this was Los Angeles, the seventies. My dad came out. I remember standing next to him. I said, 'I'm going back inside,' and he said to me, 'No, you stand right there.' I remember the look on his face. I can see it now. He looked like nothing would move him.

"Another time I came home from school and found police cars in front of the house. I started to go in and my dad told me, 'No, don't go in there.' Some White kids in the neighborhood had broken in, stolen some things and painted racial epithets on the walls. He told me what was going on. A Black man living next to White folks, that was the kind of thing that made some people upset. But that's something else he didn't fear, being a conspicuous example. He didn't hide his enthusiasms, he lived them right out in the open. He wanted only to work as hard and live as well as anyone else. He sought to be an example in everything he did, and he kept the promises he made to himself, his family and his customers. That's how he could achieve goals that some other people might have feared to set.

"That lesson sunk in. I learned never to back down or compromise out of fear. Day to day now, like anyone, I might get in situations where people want to take advantage, where people feel they can say anything. Keep in mind, I'm an African-American man in Colorado, and we make up about 5 percent of the population in the Rocky Mountain region. It happens from time to time that people might feel they can take advantage of a situation. I'm talking about in business, in life, at the bank, at the supermarket. I don't look for trouble, but it happens. My better half here is White, and it comes up occasionally that someone offers an opinion about that. From my early childhood on I've felt I'm not going to allow anyone just to say and do anything they want to do. If it comes to standing my ground, I'll do that. I have to set an example for my daughter. There are people who feel you should turn the other cheek, and I understand that. I'm a gentle man by nature. But growing up, I saw in my father how a gentle man can be a strong man, too.

"Thinking as I do might have gotten me into as much trouble as it has helped me," Pat says, "but I think you have to assume responsibility. If there's one thing I'd like to teach my child, it's that when these situations come up, you don't put your tail between your legs and run. You'll be running all your life if you do. I never saw my father run. He showed me a lot about how to live, to work, to earn what you get and enjoy it . . . but the most important thing for me was that he never ran, no matter what faced him. Life confronted him and he faced things head on.

"There are challenges every day for all of us, and most of them have nothing at all to do with race. They're about money or the future or love or health . . . fear isn't about Black or White; it isn't about what you have or where you live. You can't buy protection from it. You have to find courage inside. I have a friend who lost his ten-year-old son this past summer to a heart problem. This guy and I grew up together. I went with him to the hospital, spent the day with him waiting. There wasn't anything he could do. That must have been the hardest day of his life. It was the hardest day of mine. I never want to experience that kind of loss, and I know too many people who've felt that.

"It's a tough world, and the temptation is always there to be angry or bitter, but those are just two other names for being afraid. Fear is waiting all the time to get you. It waited for my father all his life. He never succumbed to it. And for me, my priorities are clear. I have to pick up my game to take care of my family. I can't get discouraged. I have to keep a roof over my little girl's head. I'm a dad now, man—I'd never have thought. I'm responsible. And I'm glad. Lena gives me a sense of purpose I never felt before. When I was single, and didn't have responsibilities, I probably didn't notice half the problems out there, but now . . . now I need to look without fear at every obstacle before me, from the outside or the ones I make myself, and find a way to get over them."

THE WHITEBOARD in Pat's crowded office has a to-do list for his next cooking job, a late gig at a music club in Denver that hosts national names and local bands. Big Pat's BBQ Express is a regular weekend attraction there. He's part of the family, and his photo—"Big Pat, the Barbecue Master" is featured among the staff photos on the club Web site. Pat goes over the menu with Gigi as they prepare for the job: Polish sausage and bratwurst; barbecue chicken; pork chops; brisket sandwiches; and naturally, barbecue ribs. He loads the truck with the equipment, a portable tent and iced bins of food, and hitches up a huge propane grill on a trailer, and sets out around 6 P.M. as darkness gathers.

"I got into catering because I love to cook and I like the business," Pat says as he navigates the evening rush hour. "I worked in other vending businesses doing openings for supermarkets and events for charities and corporate work, and still do that during the season. Gigi does the promotional and administrative work setting up the jobs, and I do the heavy stuff. We've made enough to grow the company, buy bigger grills and this trailer. We're doing parties and promotional work for bigger venues, business openings, doctors' offices and so on. We've done catering jobs for five hundred people.

"We draw good crowds, and I love seeing people enjoy my food. We're looking to expand, new vehicles, a prep facility . . . we're getting pretty good at it, and it's fun. This is how my dad did it too, one job at a time. We learned a lot from him. I remember him running a big crew, three or four trucks, going into places where Black people were a surprise for some people to see. He just kept on going. I run into that here— I might be out on a cleaning job or a barbecue job, and that'll raise some curiosity in a community like this. African-Americans are still a relative rarity here in Colorado. But again—I have an objective. I run a business, I have a family, and that's where my focus is. My dad was the same way. In his day, man, he was unstoppable. So am I. When you have an objective, something you need to do no matter what, you put your mind to it, and fear doesn't get in the way."

Tonight the bill at the club includes new talent and regional bands, all friends and regulars. Some of the club staff give Pat a hand as he unloads, but he totes the weighty stuff himself, five or six hundred pounds of food at least. He ices everything down and scrubs the equipment, then sets up the tent and some chairs from inside the club to make a seating area. By eight o'clock the air is full of savory smoke from the grills and music from inside. By nine, Pat is in the zone, cooking with both hands and laughing with the staff and the patrons. The bands come out to eat as they finish their sets. By eleven, Pat has cooked four hundred pounds of food.

Most of his customers go back inside to listen to a band when the night takes a different turn. Only a handful of people are around Pat's stand when three tattooed young men dressed in black leather and steel-toed boots gather near the grills.

Their heads are shaved. They wear heavy silver rings and earrings. The tattoos on their arms and the insignia on their jackets show Nazi swastikas, iron crosses and the skull and crossbones. People give them plenty of room.

The memory of recent racial violence still haunts Denver. A brawl broke out when the Ku Klux Klan held a rally on the Martin Luther King holiday not long ago. Over twenty people were arrested. The police needed nightsticks and Mace to quell the mob. More recently, a police officer and a Black immigrant were murdered by Skinheads just a few years ago. In the latter case, a teenager willingly confessed on television, saying he shot the man because he was Black and it "didn't seem like much to me." He volunteered that he wounded a woman who had tried to help the dying man.

These guys aren't here for the music. They smoke and carry cans of beer. The smiles on their faces are hard as they ask Pat about the food.

Pat is the biggest of the Massengale brothers. Whatever they have in mind, they seem startled when he comes out from behind his grills and introduces himself to them all. He asks their names. Rick, Larry and Mike, they say. "Two of my brothers are Larry and Michael," he says with a smile. The body language is easy and relaxed. Pat makes a point of putting down his tools and facing them all to shake their hands.

They ask if they can sit. Pat joins them. The Skinheads seem a little perplexed, curious about what will happen next. This wasn't what they expected.

People from inside come out one or two at a time to ask, "Hey, Pat, you okay out here?" This is a neighborhood joint where everyone gets along. People looking for trouble aren't welcome. Even members of the bands come out to check. "Hey, we're cool," Pat tells them. The Skinheads offer Pat one of the beers they're carrying. Pat declines.

Someone among the people in the club or the leather-clad men at the barbecue stand probably *wants* a fight. Pat sits calmly, refusing to let the spark ignite. The voices are low, serene. Pat might as well be talking with people from church. He stands for a moment to check his grill. A friend from inside whispers to him, "Pat, how can you talk with these punks?" "Be cool, man," Pat says, smiling. "It's under control."

By one-thirty or so the crowd is thinning. The Skinheads have been drinking beer for at least three hours. Most of Pat's friends have left. If the men have in mind to cause a problem, now would be the time. Instead even Pat doesn't expect what comes next: they keep an eye on the stand while he packs his truck. Pat is ready to head home when one of the young men walks over.

"What's your name again?"

"I'm Pat."

The man holds out his hand. "I'm Rick. I'm a Skin. But, Pat, you're all right." Everyone goes home safe.

On the drive home Pat smiles and shakes his head at the people from both sides of the confrontation that he defused. It's likely that more than one person at the club that night was armed. "Imagine what might have happened if it had gotten ugly," he says. "People get killed that way. I've seen it happen.

"Growing up in Los Angeles, I was well aware of racial divisions, even as a kid. We lived in places where there was racial strife, racial profiling, police pressure . . . I know what it's like to walk out of a party and feel bullets going by, hear the shots and the sound of somebody driving away. We lost family and friends to violence. I know how my cousins in the Black Power Movement felt, that they were risking their lives and training for violence. They were angry, like a lot of people felt angry about 'the White man.' But how could I be angry all the time if I had White friends? I grew up in a neighborhood where my friends and I were welcome in each other's homes because we could be trusted and because we gave and earned respect. We lived in areas of Los Angeles that were melting pots, so being upset constantly at some abstract idea of the White man would have made no sense when we had real White friends in our world.

"I don't feel that the Movement was wrong in all its thinking. It was a tenet of the Movement to respect unity and community, and I have a high regard for that. One of the things I always admired about my father and my uncles was how they stuck together at their work, and that they urged us to stick together as a family. My brothers have told you, I'm sure, that he'd never tolerate it if we failed to support each other or if we let our brother get in trouble. But I do wonder about the completeness of any thinking that limits your community and insulates you from other people. Insularity comes from fear. You can't make it your dwelling place.

"My family was very conscious of racial issues and racial pride, my father included. We had our strong feelings about it. What grounded us was a sense of realism—we still had to work, still had to make a living, and we all needed to find ways to adapt during those times. I don't mean acquiescing or giving in; I mean we had to find the courage and the character to seek something better than fear and anger, and to work for that in the long run. Just like tonight—a moment of fury, a moment of giving in to fear, could have cost any of us there our lives. We wanted more than that for ourselves and for the next ones to come in our family. We had goals we wanted to achieve, and if that meant getting through a racial roadblock, then that's what we needed to do. We adapted, just as I did last night. Those Skinheads weren't expecting someone calm. They wanted to provoke a reaction and they didn't get it. They didn't get my fear. They got what I wanted to give them. I didn't let them, or anyone from inside the club for that matter, set my agenda for me. At one in the morning I'm working and keeping my mind on what I need to do because I know I have to provide for my family. There's no way I can let fear get to me. I wanted to come home to my child. Nothing would keep that from happening. Sometimes you walk through the valley of the shadow of death. *You keep walking.*"

Lena is sleeping as Pat checks in before unloading the truck. He peers into the crib and fixes her blanket. "Here's my reality check right there," he whispers.

In the garage he cleans the grill and the tools. "My wife and I like being entrepreneurs," he says. "We both worked in the corporate world here in Denver, while I got my own business off the ground. We're happier being on our own. People wonder how we can go without a steady paycheck like we used to get, but think about it . . . corporate life today isn't any steadier than being out on your own. Thinking you're safe because you're in a big company is an illusion. People we know worked twenty, twenty-five years in the same place and one day, they're done. Laid off, boom.

"My family taught me that lesson years ago—I was twenty, twenty-one years old—fearless, right? Everyone that age is fearless. And I got the greatest piece of advice I ever heard from my brothers Joe and Larry. I wanted to buy this car I saw, a used Saab. Man, this car was beautiful. It had a purple flake finish, great stereo . . . mind you it didn't actually *run,* but I thought I could fix that. And oh, man, this car would have drawn the girls, I just knew it. I'd go to the dealer every day and tell him, Hey, don't sell my car. I was working here for a telecom company and I'd just gotten a raise, and so naturally I felt like I was all set. I told my brothers about getting this car.

"Joe and Larry said to me, 'Okay, Pat, that's great, get your Saab—what happens when you get laid off?' I said, 'Laid off? I just got a raise! They love me at this company!' They said, '*Right* . . . but what are you gonna fall back on if they don't love you tomorrow? What happens if you need to make a move? How is that car going to help you if you need to make a change? Is it going to be an asset or a liability if you're on your own?' Food for thought, right? So instead of getting that car, I got a van and cleaning equipment like Larry's, and started doing detailing on cars and airplanes on weekends. I never regretted that.

"See, there's the other side of being fearless. When you're twenty years old . . . you aren't thinking with your heart or your brain. Maybe that's the way a kid that age should be thinking; but if you're smart, or if someone else is smart for you, you get that mindset out of the way. A kid doesn't know enough to be respectful of circumstances and realistic about having good alternatives. That kind of fearlessness is just being blind to consequences, and you know and I know that consequences happen. You better be prepared. I wasn't afraid of the alternative because I was ready for it.

"And my brothers helped me. When I started my business, Randy came every other month or so to help. My recipe for ribs comes from Michael. Larry gave me advice about buying trucks. My brothers taught me to bid on contracts and give estimates on jobs.

"I still made mistakes. I still had failures. I'll have other ones, too. But I don't fear them. I'll learn from them, and they won't be as serious as they once were. I think the fear of failure makes a lot of people unrealistic. They get a little security and they fight to stay there even if it's a daydream. Failure happens when you test yourself, and that's what we were all taught to do. Don't fear failure, look for the times and the places where it's likely to happen and put yourself to that test. Life will challenge you no matter how hard you try to stay secure. Being ready makes all the difference. My whole family taught me that . . . don't waste time being afraid, show some flexibility. Be adaptable to what happens. Seek responsibility because that's the real reward."

It's three in the morning when Pat finally winds down. You can see the physical fatigue there, but the smile is still on his face.

"There are men out there who can shun responsibility. They won't take the chances to learn about life, put their own interests second, fail, recover and build. I was taught different—you make your bed, you lie in it. More than that . . . you make your own opportunities, better ones than the ones you see, and you do it with the best parts of who you are. My wife tells me I'm always preaching about 'doing the right thing,' but I say, 'Hey, you're my girl, and Lena's my child, and I'm responsible, bottom line.' This is the time in my life when I can stand up and be fearless for my family. It's making me a better man to embrace that."

LESSON SIX

FOCUS

Preface by Tom Cash

For more than twenty years it's been my privilege to work with students who were born with challenges. Over this time, the names of their conditions have evolved. These children are called "autistic," "developmentally disabled," "mentally retarded" or other terms intended to be useful to professionals like me who seek to help them.

When I was new at this, I respected the terminology more than I do now. The words may be helpful to teachers, but to the students, they can be limitations: imposed with the best intentions by other people, but in the end, one more obstacle for the kids to overcome. In our compassion for them, in the interest of helping, we sometimes protect them from the things we assume they cannot do. Time and time again these kids have surprised me. In the best cases, they ignore the terminology and they trample right over the limitations. They decide for themselves who they are.

In some ways, I feel I know less than I used to about the challenges my students face, and I know that many others in the field feel as humbled as I do. The causes of developmental disorders are almost as ambiguous today as they were when I started my career. The experts predict an "epidemic" of millions of new cases in the next few years. And while a whole new population of "autistic" children is diagnosed, the diagnostic terminology is only general. It stops at *every individual. Every case is unique. Every child might exceed every expectation.*

The greatest hope these kids have is themselves, if they are permitted to feel that hope. If there is a constant in the changing understanding we have about conditions like autism, it's the spirits of the kids themselves. Resilient, eager to learn, funny, loving, these children are more creative and capable than any of us might once have imagined. They're also much stronger than we once realized, and given the chance to show that strength, they share it generously with their teachers and with each other.

I started as a teacher, but over the years I have grown into the work by becoming a student myself. The lesson these kids have taught me is never to focus my efforts on fitting them to the name of their condition, but instead, to aim higher. I don't tell them what they cannot do. I help them tell me what they can *do.*

The "epidemic" of autism and developmental disorders is just an awakening on the part of the rest of us to how common these conditions have been all along. It offers us all an opportunity to understand people who are every bit as human, and many of whom are every bit as capable, as the rest of us, and to grow with them so that we can all exceed ourselves.

Every day, I meet parents like Joe Massengale and students like his son Andre, seemingly average people who might live next door to you, who believed in themselves, took risks, failed and recovered, stayed focused and outgrew every label life might have placed on them. They remind me again and again that there is no label strong enough to lock up the human spirit.

Tom Cash earned his master's degree from California State University, Los Angeles. A longtime entrepreneur, his primary interest is children with special needs. He has taught special education students in the Los Angeles area since 1967.

Focus was the key. But the truth is, my father taught me everything: how to work, how to think, how to be neat, how to take my time and speak well. I got all that from him. My father built me.

ON A typical Sunday, Joe Massengale and Andre, his youngest son, attend services together at the Figueroa Church of Christ in South Central Los Angeles. A short drive from the neighborhood where Joe first lived, this church is among the biggest congregations in the city. Like his father, Hugh, Joe is a lifelong member of the Church of Christ. He has been part of Figueroa for over fifty years.

Joe and Andre often come to services in identical tailored suits: the father in his seventies, gray-haired, slightly bow-legged in his walk, smiling and shaking hands with friends; the son, fifty years younger, slim, immaculately neat with a trim mustache like Joe's, hair clipped short, bright-eyed and smiling. They take seats in front, and stand together during the two-hour service singing the old hymns Hugh Massengale sang back in East Texas. Neither one needs to read the words.

People here often remark on the bond between these men, but then, that bond shows everywhere they go. Joe and Andre see each other nearly every day, working all over Los Angeles, running errands together, eating breakfast at Joe's. Andre calls his father early every morning to find out how he is and what he needs.

Andre Massengale was born in Los Angeles shortly before Joe's second marriage ended. Joe lived in Fallbrook most of the time until Andre was about ten years old; there wasn't the chance for him to see his youngest son daily, as he had the other five. And there was another challenge: Andre was diagnosed with a mild developmental disability, a form of autism, so it was sometimes a struggle for him to communicate. Even worse for Joe, Andre was actually afraid of his father. There was no good reason for it, but the man with the truck who stopped by often to visit frightened Andre enough to make the little boy run and hide.

Things that come easy for his brothers—conversation, laughter, reminiscences of the past and anticipations of a great future—are for Andre things that were earned through hard work, and of which he is justly proud. Now approaching thirty, Andre may have come the farthest of all the Massengale sons. He and Joe made that journey together, and the story of this part of Joe's life is inseparable from that of his son.

IN THE kitchen of Joe's house on a spring day, Andre and Joe have changed out of their work coveralls and both wear clean sweats. Andre has been there since first light. He drives over in his new silver pickup, a twin of Joe's, and manicures the lawn by hand, weeding, fertilizing, packing the roots around the ficus trees.

When asked what single lesson his father gave him, Andre doesn't hesitate: "Focus is the main one. Focus was the key. But the truth is, my father taught me everything. How to work, how to think, how to be neat, how to take my time and speak well. I got all that from him." He pauses to emphasize the point: "My father *built* me.

"When I was a kid in the 1980s, and I lived with my mother and grandmother, my dad would pull up to the house in his pickup," Andre remembers. "I didn't know him well. I was afraid of him. I just wanted him to go home.

"I was a mischievous kid, like all kids. I'd pull sprinkler heads off people's lawns and put them in the trash. I'd play with things I shouldn't have. Childish stuff. That's when my father took me in hand. He showed me how to focus myself, how to work, how to concentrate. 'You just have to focus on what you're doing,' that's what he told me. I have to keep my mind on my business, say what I have to say; talk as much as I need to and not more. He showed me how to pay attention to what I'm doing. He showed me how to take care of myself, how to feel happy. My dad is a great man."

In resuming his business in Los Angeles, Joe had a few reliable clients to build on, but not enough to stay busy. He was starting pretty much from scratch. His old crew was off with other companies, and the first five Massengale sons were away at school or starting their careers. To reestablish Joe's Expert Tree Service, Joe was back selling door-to-door, and this time, he was sixty years old and working alone. He took the second bedroom in Michael's Los Angeles apartment and went out from there first thing every morning just as he had as a rookie forty years before.

Andre lived with his mother a few blocks away. In his early years, it became clear that his condition might affect not only his relationships with his father and brothers, but his whole future. Joe faced a double challenge: rebuilding his fortune and bridging the divide with his son.

ANDRE'S CASE was probably a mild version of a disorder that remains mysterious to the medical profession. Much progress has been made in understanding and treating it. As it used to be understood, it was, in the words of one investigator, a "death sentence" to the child who had it.

"Autism" is so broad and general a term that it is inadequate as a description of the condition that affects a person's development. Autistic children grow mentally in unpredictable spurts and plateaus through their early years. They think in their own ways, often in pictures or images. Some notice only colors or shapes. Noises and unexpected stimuli can be extremely upsetting. Some seem unable to remember anything about other people. Figures of speech and analogies can be especially difficult to follow. They can hear the language spoken by their parents, but it does not register with them as the parents intend it to, so the same words or ideas can seem different to them from instance to instance. They can repeat language like a recording, but the meaning gets lost, so teaching them concepts like shame, consequences, sharing, friendship, is hard. Slow to talk, disinterested in sharing the kind of discovery-learning that most children delight in, autistic kids often cocoon themselves in a world of their own making.

Autism is present in all races, all over the world. Mystifying and difficult to treat, the condition is known to be widespread in the United States, but estimates of the true incidence range from 1 in 166 to 1 in 2,500 children, depending in part on how broadly defined it is. Improving diagnostic techniques and changes in the evaluative criteria for it contribute to, but still do not explain, an alarming rise in the number of cases. The word "epidemic" appears in articles in major newspapers and Web sites associated with remedial agencies.

The fact is, no one knows for certain what causes autism. There is no preemptive test for it. It must appear in a child in order to be diagnosed. And there is no known universal treatment.

Autism and related developmental disabilities are at last emerging from decades of mistaken theories and ineffective treatments. Luckily, as the number of people affected has grown, so has a new body of scientific knowledge about it. In Andre Massengale's time, old theories about emotionally distant parents or inoculations as a cause have been replaced by theories about genetic predispositions and environmental factors. One encouraging discovery is that the word "autism" is not a one-size-fits-all diagnosis. In recent years a new appreciation has arisen for fine gradations on the scale from nearly normal to severe, and this has given new hope to people who might once have fallen under a label that did not accurately describe them.

The bond Andre shares with his father and brothers might

not be possible in severe autistics. The capacity to share such a bond might have been lost to Andre, even with his mild version, had they not worked so hard to make it real. In cases like Andre's, relationships are often the biggest challenge. Many people feel as Andre did—they don't feel deprived or alone, and they might be indifferent to the company of loved ones. Like Andre once felt, they just want other people to go home.

Andre, "high functioning" on the scale, was naturally bright and inquisitive. He had what he needed to grow, learn and flourish with the right training opportunities. If there was a single overriding lesson Joe Massengale wanted to teach all his sons, it was that no label could confine them. They were free to be the men they wanted to be, if they worked at it. That included Andre.

LAURIE STEPHENS, PH.D., is director of the Autism Spectrum Disorders Program for The Help Group in Los Angeles. A privately funded nonprofit supported by some of the city's most famous names and companies, they help children across a very broad spectrum of cases at four beautiful campuses.

"The definition of 'autism' has broadened so much recently," Dr. Stephens says, "that I can say the word and mean something almost completely different from someone else, and we can both be correct. There are many more points along the spectrum within the broad definition that we used to understand. That means new prospects for treatment and understanding.

"Years ago, the word meant only a severely impaired person

who was potentially mentally retarded, with behavioral problems, no functional skills, communications problems and no real prospects for a normal adult life. We understand much more now, and we know that people living with the condition can marry, have careers and raise families. In some cases they're brilliant, leaders in their fields. They might be thought of as eccentric or quirky; they might have unusual aspects in their personalities; but they can cope and adapt. The fact is, we all have eccentricities and quirks. We all exhibit behaviors like rituals and thinking in methodical sequences just like the kind of behaviors autistics exhibit. There's a much finer line in many cases between "normal" and "not normal" than we used to think. What makes these people different is that they need to learn with more training how to be aware of those things and handle them. That's a challenge, but more and more, it is possible.

"We know much more then ever about what *doesn't* cause autism spectrum disorders," Dr. Stephens continues. "A compromised immune system, vaccinations, the old 'refrigerator mother' theory that a neglectful parent was behind it . . . those are largely obsolete ideas now.

"We're still investigating the causes, and now it seems clear that there probably is no single basis. There might be a range of factors underlying the condition: genetics; new environmental factors. Our understanding in that area is growing all the time. The point is, there is greater hope than ever. So the label should not be a 'death sentence' anymore.

"Insofar as we can generalize about it," she says, "people living with this condition face a triad of challenges:

"First: they have language or communication difficulties.

Autistic kids often have problems with delayed language. Some don't speak until relatively late in their childhoods, and they may have used language they've memorized without truly understanding what it means, in the way an American child might learn to sing 'Frère Jacques' by sound, without understanding the meaning of the words. So there is this broad continuum of language problems, with the denominator being that the autistic child finds it hard to converse. Language is often empty for them. The mechanics of conversation they understand, but they don't understand abstraction, nuance, humor, inference, a real exchange of ideas between minds. And the language itself doesn't help because English is evolving all the time, with new colloquialisms, figures of speech, new expressions. Being a literal thinker, someone with this condition might find it confusing if you said, 'I'm running in circles' or 'Picture this.' They're likely to take such a turn of phrase literally and wonder what you mean.

"Second: they have social difficulties, ranging from the kids who have no interest at all in socializing to kids who are desperate to have friends but have no idea how to do it. The latter type can be intrusive and demanding without knowing it. They might talk too much, or too little; and they just don't get the reciprocity of relationships. A big part of the social deficit for many is what we call the deficit of a Theory of Mind, which is the capacity to intuit another person's mental state by reading facial or body language. This is a basic social skill, and an enormous component of socializing. Autistic kids are missing that. They can be oblivious to people, and to most of the little cues and signals that make up the basis of interactions.

"That's the third factor they face, a limited behavioral repertoire: limited interests, repetitiveness of routine. They like being rigid. They like sequences and strict habits in even the most mundane things like eating or dressing. They ritualize to the point where any deviation from the ritual can be extremely disturbing to them. And often, they assume that if they're passionately enthusiastic about a thing, so are you. If they know about it, you must want to know about it, and they can't fathom that you might not share their interest. That's another cruel difficulty of this—being isolated socially by your enthusiasms. Some kids retreat into their interests and stay there. They get passionately devoted to a single thing, and they want to pay attention to nothing else. It could be anything; planes, stamps, numbers, a single toy. It becomes the world for them.

"The habits of the syndrome are easy to slip into, so we remind our students all the time about the simple things they can do to build new habits, positive ones that go counter to the instinct they have to isolate themselves. Some of our kids keep printed cards on their desks that say MAKE EYE CONTACT. Use your eyes to share interests and not just your wants. The point of all this is, the mind can be exercised, and the social skill that was weak when they were on their own gets strengthened. They can learn to keep the understanding they gain, and with time, they can start responding on their own.

"The steps might be harder, but they can be taken. And success in this area dramatically increases their chance for personal freedom and autonomy as people leading productive, happy lives.

"We're just now figuring out how to research autism at

very early ages," Dr. Stephens says. "It's become easier to find them because we recognize patterns in families. There seems to be a genetic predisposition in families for it, and if there's an autistic sibling it's more likely there will be another and we can help the family intervene early with good effects."

The facility where Dr. Stephens helps her kids is beautiful, staffed with a high ratio of counselors and teachers to students and equipped with the best classrooms and learning aids. Sadly, care at this level is the exception and not the rule.

For all the progress being made, effective treatment for autistic children, particularly for the severely autistic, lags behind the learning. The father of an autistic child wrote in *The New York Times* of the hope he felt at seeing his own son's success, but continues, "James's progress has a sadder side: that he has been such an exception. Not everybody who gets the treatment he did progresses so far, although some go further. But only a relative handful of children with autism are thought to receive even the minimum standard of care, a pattern reflected in an increase in requests for institutional placements as the leading edge of last decade's cases reaches adolescence." He continued, "[James] is one of 150,000 or more American children classified in the last decade as having the once-rare disorder, including 25,000 in 2003. Half a century ago, polio epidemics left perhaps 5,000 children a year with some degree of disability, and the sight of children stricken overnight galvanized the nation. But autism's arrival, and the response to it, has not been so dramatic."

For a child who feels instinctively that he or she is different, out of place, out of step in a social setting, any interaction can be a fearful risk. The child who hears the word "autism," even from someone with good intentions, is hearing a misunderstood label. They may feel they have no choice but to accept the idea that they are odd, unwanted and incapable. They could easily fall into the trap of believing that they have no prospects, and that they are wrong to hope for simple happiness as they see it in other people's lives. The effect can be just as traumatic on their families.

DURING JOE Massengale's lifetime, the era called the "dark ages" of treating such conditions, a diagnosis of autism might have been a sentence to lifelong confinement. During his own lifetime, Andre Massengale's true potential might have gone unfulfilled.

No matter how rapid and encouraging the advances being made at the forefront of research, this progress still does not reach down into the typical family being affected by these disorders. The average child still lives with the risks of disappearing into the system, of being diagnosed incorrectly or not at all; of experiencing ostracism or bullying; of feeling alone and wounded by something beyond his control. Many doctors do not administer the tests that help recognize the problem. Others are reluctant to make the diagnosis of autism, and instead reassure the parents that the child could outgrow the symptoms. Increasingly, researchers see that early diagnosis is the key to successful intervention. The better the condition is understood in the early stages—as early as three to six months—the more effective the training can be to give the child a fighting chance. But many children wait months to be examined, and years for treatment. The opportunity for every possible measure of improvement lessens, day by day, like sand in an hourglass.

In the worst case, says Dr. Stephens, "children with this challenge face adult life in isolation. Unemployed, living with their families if they can, or homeless if all else fails, they're vulnerable to behaviors that they cannot control but which society cannot permit. Many of them do things with no ill intent for which they might be arrested and prosecuted, and the victims and courts can be unsympathetic to their condition. Such people might not understand that one doesn't just walk into someone else's home, or touch someone inappropriately. Anger and frustration lead to more isolation, more anger and frustration.

"You don't have to live out the worst-case scenario to suffer from the effects of this. Imagine being a bright young person with an undiagnosed case of this condition, or an improperly understood case. You have trouble making friends, or you don't want friends at all. You're an outsider; you don't have a feel for how people think and act even in your own family. You feel rejected, alone and depressed. Your attempts to share yourself and your interests with people fail. You get teased and harassed. The condition alone, even a mild instance, isn't the worst thing in your life. The worst thing is the effects it has on your world. Those might make a person feel that the best they can ask for is a life tinged with seclusion and loneliness."

ANDRE WAS much better off than many children with his affliction. When Joe moved back to Los Angeles, Andre was living in the same neighborhood in a good home with Joe's ex-wife and her other children. The opportunity was there, if it could be taken, to help Andre make a dramatic transformation in his life.

Michael Massengale was the one who bridged the relationship between his father and his youngest brother.

"It worried me that Andre was growing up so close by, but didn't feel like he was part of the family," Michael says. "This was my stepbrother and I didn't really know him. I'd go by and try to see him, but we couldn't communicate. He'd start crying when any of us were around him, and he'd never let my dad come near him. One day I went over to his house with my dad and we took him out for a walk. He wasn't more then ten, and he seemed just panicked. 'Andre, can you just walk with us?' I said. 'Just come take a walk.' He was walking and crying, very upset, but we had to get him through this. My dad was being very gentle, trying just to communicate, and finally as we got back to the house, he said, 'Andre, come over to the truck for a moment.'

"Dad's landscaping truck was parked by the curb. Dad showed Andre all the tools, one by one, saws and pruning poles and clippers, putting each one in Andre's hands. Maybe he didn't know what else to try. But—it was as though a window opened between them. I think that was Andre's first glimpse of himself with something to do, a real task, and a way to show what he could be. From that moment on, they were inseparable.

"The next day Andre went to work with Dad, and it

changed both their lives. Dad got him a uniform. He was thrilled with it. He came over every day on weekends and in the summer. 'Dad, let's go to work. Come on, let's go to work.' It focused him. It gave him a sense of who he was—he wasn't tossed into a category anymore with a label on him. He wasn't 'disabled' and he wasn't 'autistic.' He was Andre Massengale and he was a *man*.

"Our whole lives," Michael says, "my brothers and I weren't allowed to make excuses about what was in the way— you just never brought any excuses up around my dad. 'Something's hard? Sorry to hear that, you better get to work.' No excuses. My dad was always like that with the five older brothers. Now it was Andre, ten years old, doing that to *him*. 'Come on, Dad, let's go to work. You're broke? You're sixty? Sorry to hear it, let's get to work.' More than anything else, it was Andre that got my father going again."

Andre's motivation might have been as simple as the desire for his own swimming pool. He told his mother he wanted one, and she relayed the request to Joe. Joe's response was predictable: if he wants one, he'd better be ready to work for it. Andre took the order seriously enough to drag a pick into his backyard and start digging a pool himself. The practical compromise was going out with his father on landscaping jobs.

"I took right to it," Andre remembers with a smile. "It was awesome—I liked it from the first day, and I was good at it from the beginning. I remember the first job we did, cleaning up a garden with bird-of-paradise flowers and banana trees. I loved it. It's hard work, but it's fun, and my dad was always around to help me understand what to do. I just liked it so much, being good at something. I liked earning his respect. I liked being out on the road with him, even when it was hot in the summer. He always took good care of me. And it changed my mind about the swimming pool—I filled the hole back in! I didn't need it anymore because I was learning, even so young, to take care of myself and be independent, and that was what I valued most."

Joe had no idea that his youngest son would leap so enthusiastically at the work. "I kept him busy with light work that first day," he says, "just to watch him, and he completely surprised me. He was *fastidious*. You could see how proud it made him, being out there in his uniform raking and weeding; he was just tireless. I knew right then, he had an appetite for the work. It mattered to him to do it right. That showed me a lot about him, and a lot about what he wanted to be. He wasn't but ten or eleven, and he wanted to do the work of a man twice his age. He wasn't going to make excuses or let something stand in his way. It gave him a purpose.

"At the end of his first day, I gave him twenty-five dollars in one-dollar bills. I guess that must have looked good to a ten-year-old—next day at seven A.M., there was Andre knocking on my door: 'Let's go to work.'

"He spent the summer with me, getting better and better at it, and when he started school again, he worked a lot of weekends. Soon we started going further and further out of town, out to Palm Springs and down to San Diego, road trips like I used to do, and he took right to that.

"He was the one who started suggesting those out-of-town trips. 'Come on, Dad, let's go find a job.' We spent hours in the truck. We got time to talk on those long rides, and we got to share something I didn't expect. And a friendship just grew between us. The more time we spent together, the closer we got. He was a thoughtful young man. He was observant. He was much more aware of things than anyone had ever given him credit for. My customers loved him from the first time they met him. He was as polite and gracious a young man as anyone ever met, and he was as attentive to detail as any man twice his age. It made me proud every time they greeted him. They trusted him like they trusted me."

The pleasure Andre takes in the work shows in his eyes as he walks around the lawn of his father's house. "I loved the kind of work my dad was doing," he says. "He showed me everything: how to take care of the tools, how to be careful using them, about safety goggles and keeping an eye on what other people are doing. You have to take it seriously. Landscaping is dangerous, and I was brought up to be careful because you never can tell what's going to happen. No one on my dad's crew has ever been hurt seriously, and I won't because I'm careful. It's a way for me to stay focused, and it's taught me a lot about responsibility, about paying attention to detail. If you understand those things, you can be more independent. That's a great thing to know."

▦

"I KNEW what it meant to have a label on you," Joe says. "It doesn't matter what it is, or whether it's a fact or not. People back when I was a kid said things to me that were intended to tell me who I was and what I could do. 'Get off the sidewalks,' 'Niggers shouldn't be driving a wagon at night,' all that. That wasn't right. I didn't let the labels make any difference in my own life, and I wasn't about to let a label tell Andre what he could make of himself."

Tom Cash, a lifelong educator in the Los Angeles city and county school systems, got to know Andre not long after Joe returned from Fallbrook.

"I met Andre when he was about ten. He was one of the kids in my special ed class," Tom says. "He was a wonderful kid, highly intelligent, personable, friendly and curious. He had a sweet kind of impishness. He liked attention. He was playful. You could see the aptitude there in him waiting to be nurtured. Years ago he'd have been classified 'educable mentally retarded,' but that description never mattered. What matters is that he's at the very high end of the spectrum, and he had innate coping skills and comprehension, plus the things Joe was giving him through experiential learning.

"If anyone on earth is gifted at reading people and understanding the nuances of personal interaction, it's Joe Massengale. For him it was a survival skill. Joe is a master of adapting to circumstances while keeping the core of his character. He didn't compromise himself, but he was very flexible to the situations he was in and to the things he needed to do. It's how he prospered all those years in a business that started with knocking on a stranger's door in places where he wasn't welcome. Most adults don't read people anywhere near as well as Joe does. So he was the perfect man to teach Andre."

Tom is quick to dispense with the word "autistic." "A diagnosis in the professional community can be like summary justice somewhere else," he says. "It should be the beginning of improvement; but the clinical term heard in the wrong place and at the wrong time can be a reason for the person himself to give up hope for improvement. If a person were to hear a word like 'autistic' and he believes himself to *be* autistic, with possibly the most severe cases as his only frame of reference, there's every chance he'll believe the worst about himself, and give up then and there.

"We have kids in my school today who are nearly normal in most respects. We have others who will require care and supervision every day of their lives. They are individuals, not one label. They can't look at one another and find common weaknesses under some umbrella term. The have to find their own uniqueness and their own strength.

"I call it 'acquired helplessness.' It happens to everybody. Anyone is vulnerable—anyone who's ever felt like an outsider, like a second-class citizen, knows that feeling. The courage it takes to feel as though you're really in charge of your life can vanish from us all, anytime, and in some cases it never comes back. A single word can do it. It can be a slur like the ones Joe grew up with. If he'd believed what he heard when people told him he didn't merit equality and prosperity and the basics of a decent life, he might have believed he was helpless. It might have constrained his thinking for the rest of his life. He never let that happen to himself, and he wouldn't permit Andre ever to feel helpless. Joe gave his son love, but not breaks. He gave Andre trust and patience and support, but he never babied him. And Andre thrived. You could watch it happen. Andre loved getting his father's approval. He strove to win it.

"Joe taught Andre survival skills he'll use his whole life to read situations and trust himself in them," Tom says. "Here's an example—Joe took Andre to driver's education here in Los Angeles. *That's* how much faith Joe had in his son. Lots of parents in that position wouldn't have considered doing that—plenty of perfectly normal people are afraid to drive in L.A.—and they'd try to protect their kids from it. Andre is as fastidious at the wheel as he is anywhere else, and he knows his way around town as well as anyone, so Joe's faith is vindicated. Andre is mobile and employable and proud to be independent. He's learned though experiencing again and again all the things he needs to cope with day-to-day living. Joe has given him a great gift in that regard, the emotional stability to handle life on his own, and not only that, but life in one of the busiest, most challenging places in the world."

JOE MAY have found intuitively what many teachers seek for kids like Andre. Many versions of the behavioral therapies being tried today for impaired kids feature the same things Andre found on the job: close attention, fast feedback, long hours, physical and mental tests, deadlines and tangible rewards. As with all the sons raised in Joe's business, Andre could take immediate pride in the job well done. A spotless yard, praise from his co-workers and the clients—they learned quickly to look for him when Joe came, and they asked about him on days he didn't work—and good pay for good work all have counterparts in the classroom training and clinical therapies now being widely sought by educators and parents.

Tom Cash feels that putting Andre to work was the best thing Joe could have done for him.

"Every loving parent has the instinct to protect a child, and to provide them with an excuse for what they can't do. With the best intentions, parents want to spare their kids pain; they want to protect their kids from the suffering or hardship they went through; they want to give their kids everything. What they're doing is teaching a warped sense of values and behavior. I see many parents doing all they can for their disabled kids, and after a while the kids learn to get the parents to do everything. Parents actually feel guilty for the child's condition and they're eager to compensate for it as a way to lift the blame. *You cannot compensate*. Life is what it is. The kids need to use what they have, not deny it.

"Joe won't have anything to do with guilt or compensation," Tom says. "He did no coddling with his sons. He strengthened them. It's like I tell parents, 'Life isn't a guided tour; it's a journey.' Joe provided a map of character and discipline and focus to his sons that would take them wherever they wanted to go, but he didn't make the trip for them. He knew he'd never be able to prevent bad things from happening; they happen. What he could do is prepare Andre to deal effectively with it.

"Joe has given Andre constant proof that he can do what the label 'autistic' suggests is impossible, that he shouldn't ever feel limited by it. The method was trial and error, and that's a process many people fear because they fear failure. Joe taught Andre not to fear it. He let Andre fail, and let him get back up to try again.

"That's a very liberating thing," Tom says, "because a sense of self-worth is critical to any prolonged course of therapy. It's critical for *life*. Life is much more about recovery than it is about success. Anyone might succeed, and people who do it too easily doubt their success. But everyone fails, and you don't doubt success once you know failure. Andre knows he's earned his success. Nothing can ever take that away from him. He's always working to get better, just as Joe is. They both give 200 percent all the time. It really is gratifying to watch them together. They have a fantastic relationship with deep liking and respect as well as that powerful love. They keep finding ways to stretch themselves, to try new things and take risks. And the driver of that is the same for them both: that powerful faith in themselves.

"Kids have to fail to succeed. Joe put Andre in a position where he could test himself, fail if he had to, and recover and appreciate what it took inside him to get back up. Joe showed him the path. The lessons Joe gave him were the best ones a father could give a son: You can learn. You can grow. You have the help and support you need. And you can rely first of all on yourself.

"You are *free*."

IT TOOK Joe just a few months to get on his feet again, and within a year he was in a new home, with a new crew and some new horses in his stable. He was back. The best part of his recovery was the unexpected bonus he got from Andre.

"He gave me a chance to experience being a father in a way

I never had before," Joe says. "There was *time* with Andre. It didn't feel so urgent. We could talk in a way that hadn't been possible for me before. I honestly didn't expect it to happen. I was ready for the worst, for my own son not wanting me to be part of his life. But when Andre showed an interest in me, well, I just went in all the way.

"I think that Andre pulled me back up from where I was. I'd get low sometimes . . . many days I didn't want to go to work, but he did. 'Come on, Dad, let's find some work.' I'd go by and pick him up just to spend the time with him, even if I didn't think we'd find anything. And we'd drive around for hours, pick a street, knock on doors, and maybe get a job. He was inspiring to me because even as a little kid, he just didn't quit."

More than just the work, the experience of getting to know his youngest son gave Joe a chance to discover something he might have missed with the older ones. Michael Massengale detected it in watching the two become close. "With the rest of us, my dad had to concentrate on just keeping us alive. He could never take that for granted with five boys growing up together in Los Angeles at that time. He had to show us how to *survive*. And he couldn't be easy on us. He couldn't be our friend. Working together in a hazardous business, living together and getting through school without getting into trouble: it meant that he had to be very firm with us. With Andre, there might have been a little less pressure on him, and he could enjoy the experience of being a father more. He could find the peaceful side of his own strength, the gentle parts of it, because those were the things Andre needed most."

Michael is right. You can hear the wonder in Joe's voice

when he talks about getting up in the middle of the night in a Palm Springs motel room after a long day in the desert heat to wipe his little boy's face with a cool towel. He couldn't indulge himself that way while being the disciplinarian for five rowdy boys. Andre permitted him that new feeling.

"I had to be an authority figure for my other sons. Five boys, no women in the house, Los Angeles . . . Man, you better had keep an eye on them, because they didn't need to look for trouble. Trouble would look for them if they weren't careful. I know they felt that way, that I was tough and demanding with them, but I felt they needed that. With Andre, I found a different side of myself. He needed an opportunity to shine, not authority. He needed approval, and he was willing to earn it in ways that surprised me all the time. He didn't want any breaks. I didn't have any plan for it. I had no idea what would happen. I didn't know if he'd even like it. But he was my son and I couldn't just give up. I'd seen men grow into experts from boys who didn't know what to do, so I knew what could happen. But he exceeded everything I could ever have hoped for.

"Maybe it's that both of us started with nothing—people would have laughed at him and expected he'd never amount to anything, the same as they used to do to me back when I was a hungry kid in Marshall. I never asked to be treated differently because my family didn't have anything, I just asked to prove myself. He was exactly the same way. He never said, 'I can't.' "

And Andre's presence rejuvenated the business. Now Joe got a double satisfaction out of leaving a yard in perfect shape; he could see how his son blossomed a little every time they went out together. "The two of us would take on jobs I used to do with a full crew," he says, smiling. "I was sixty-five years old and I was doing high work in trees again. Man, that was hard! But Andre kept me going. We never let each other down. He says I taught him focus; I'd say he helped me find my own again when I might have lost it. I saw the respect he got even when he was so young. People could see how earnest he was, how serious about doing his best, and they loved seeing him, and I'll tell you, nothing motivated me more than that. I started working again for a few of my old customers, and it wasn't long before business picked up. The reason was Andre. I'm sure he was the key to me getting back on my feet. He helped me keep my own focus and stay optimistic. He had a chance to shine, and so did I. It was a miracle for us both."

The pleasure they took in being together only deepened as Andre grew into manhood. The work they share is an apt metaphor for the devotion they feel for each other. These men cultivate each other.

How does it make Andre feel? "Awesome," he says. "Really awesome. I like everything it does for me."

Joe smiles too. "When Andre had saved himself a nice little nest egg, I asked him about the swimming pool. By then he'd lost interest—he wanted to work more than he wanted to have that pool. He's a guy who can take care of himself. If I died today there's no way anyone could talk Andre into doing something wrong. He's too strong, too much in charge of himself. He's different from anyone else I ever met. He has such a great attitude. In my wildest dreams I never thought he'd turn out so well."

Andre graduated from high school and celebrated the traditional way, by attending his senior prom. Michael drove Joe's limo as Andre's chauffeur that night.

"Andre wore a tux, naturally. He looked great. I had on a blue suit, and we drove over to pick up his date. Man, this young woman answered the door—I'm talking a knockout. A beautiful girl. Lane is her name. She's a doctor today. I said, 'Whoa . . . here's my kid brother taking the prettiest girl in school.' I asked him, 'Andre, how'd you get Lane to go to the prom with you?' He just said, '*I decided*.' "

ANDRE STANDS and stretches on Joe's front lawn, pleased at last with the way it looks. "My father's happy with my work and that makes me feel proud. And I love taking care of him. I love supporting him because he's done so much for me. Little things like keeping the tools organized, making sure we have drinks in the cold box; those things matter. I like paying attention to the details that make a job go well. He says I'm his right arm and that means a lot to me."

He stops to pick up a last stray leaf. "I keep awake. I keep my mind together. I stay focused because it's important to take care of the clients we have. Our clients all know what they can expect from us. You have to stay focused for that. Today we started together around 7:30 and finished late in the morning. We went grocery shopping and I helped him put the groceries away. I love to help him, I really do.

"My dad and I have been all over Southern California

working together. It's a great way to learn. It's taught me things I need to know—how to be careful, to be flexible and to pay attention. Because of him I have money in the bank and I can take care of myself. And it makes me proud to know that clients like me and look for me."

Andre stays in touch with his brothers and with family all over the country, and in doing so, he has conquered another facet of his condition. He knows he's part of the family and he makes sure to play the same role they all play in supporting, advising and encouraging each other.

THE LAST obstacle Andre and Joe had to overcome together is one we all must face.

"He was maybe sixteen or so, and we were together in the truck," Joe remembers. "I made a passing remark about not being around forever. He asked me what I meant. I tried to explain to him that none of us lives forever, even if we want to.

"He got terribly upset. He was just inconsolable. I couldn't mention anything like that for a long time. But he has to be ready. I can do a lot to help him, but I need him to know he'll be on his own someday, and that he can be truly independent. So for a while, when someone from our church would pass, he and I would go together to the funeral service, and I'd try very carefully to help him understand what it meant. I think he does. I think he'll be ready. He has a future now. A label could have taken that away from him. He won it back for himself."

Finished at last on the front lawn, Andre comes in and

washes up. He embraces his father before he gets ready to leave.

"My dad is a great man," Andre says. "He taught me everything. And we've done a lot for each other."

"He's right about that," says Joe. "Andre is my right arm. My left one too."

AFTERWORD

INVESTMENT

Preface by B. Michael Young

I was twenty-three, two years into the "real world" after graduating from Howard University, and a member of the Washington, D.C., chapter of the National Urban League of Young Professionals when I attended their seminar for first-time home buyers. The chapter promoted the talk as part of a series on the subject of empowerment, but like just about everyone there, I went expecting only to learn a few things about buying a house. I did, but that was just the beginning.

The speaker discussed practical issues like the importance of a good credit rating and a balanced budget. He walked us through the steps one needs to take to be a home buyer: contact a lender, obtain a pre-qualification letter, meet with a real estate agent, search the computer database for properties that meet your criteria and fall within your price range, visit each house, select a house, and then apply for the loan.

For a young man at the start of his career, all these things seemed a little daunting. Until that time, I had only lived in one house, the house that I called "home" for the first eighteen years of my life. Thereafter it was all dorms and apartments. I listened with a daydream in my mind about having my first really comfortable place, with the luxuries I thought were the basics of adulthood. What broke my reverie was hearing the presenter say to us all that he wasn't just talking about buying a house. He was instructing us all about making our first major investment.

Think about the real meaning of that word. Think about the meaning of some of the terms you'll hear along with it: improvement, interest, obligation, capital, value. You'll hear them when you're making all the most important decisions you make in business, in marriage and in raising your children.

As I thought about these ideas, I could feel my daydream change into something I hadn't anticipated. Instead of looking ahead into an imaginary house with wall-to-wall carpets, three bedrooms and new appliances, I looked into myself, into my feelings and attitudes about who I am and what I really had to invest. At that moment, the whole idea of investment stopped being just about money or property. These other words started taking on new significance, too. Improvement: not just putting in a new lawn, but improving myself, my expectations and my performance. Interest: what was my best interest, and what were the interests of people I care for? What are my obligations to myself, my community, my family? What obligations did I really want to seek, and to fulfill? What beyond money was the capital I needed to commit, and what did I hope to gain that was truly of value?

We all face questions like this every day, because, as I realized in that seminar, all decisions are investments. I don't mean just major ones. I mean even the ones you make casually. They all matter. They all have returns, good or bad. That's what's real about the "real world." The obvious investment decisions are financial: buy a new car or fix the old one? Big house, or modest one? Other decisions are harder to weigh in dollar amounts, but they are even more important because the capital involved is far more precious than money. We all have hopes and dreams for ourselves and the people we love. We can all make those dreams real. But how do we make that happen?

Start with this: Time is capital. Interest is what is truly important to you. Obligation is the promise you make to stretch yourself, aim high and keep your integrity. Value is the return you get, and what you share with your family and your community. Investment is what you do with your time, every day.

Look into yourself and ask, What are the best investments I can make? What will I need to make that investment become real? You'll need confidence to begin. Fortitude to learn and fail and grow. Persistence to keep pushing when it's all uphill. Pride to draw on your deepest resources when nothing else is there for you. Fearlessness to recognize all the bad possibilities clearly and confront them head-on. And focus to continually check, refine and improve.

Whether you want to build a life, a business or a family, these are the assets that turn a dream into a reality. The lessons you see here are empowering examples of how others did this, but your own journey is the real point of this book.

The capital you need to build for the future is already yours.

Invest wisely.

B. Michael Young is president of the National Urban League of Young Professionals. He was recently selected by America Online Black Voices as one of the top ten young civil rights leaders in the country. In 1997 *Ebony* magazine recognized and profiled Young as one of the "Top 30 Young Leaders of the Future" under the age of thirty.

LIKE HUNDREDS of towns in America today, Marshall, Texas, balances the distinctive remnants of its past with the franchise stores and restaurants that standardize the country from coast to coast.

Today, its top priority is attracting new investment to rebuild the job base and renew the city's economy. State and local preservationists work diligently to save the best of Marshall's nineteenth-century heritage while trying to give the twenty-first century a home.

The question is: What is the best?

Antebellum Marshall lives on in about a hundred historical markers placed around town by the Texas Historical Commission. Many of the most beautiful old houses are bed-and-breakfast places. Over a dozen of the town's irreplaceable homes, churches and municipal buildings are on the National Register of Historic Places. Some are being restored. Some are being given new identities. The Hotel Marshall, where Joe Massengale worked shining shoes, and where he got the news of his father's passing, is just a shell, with every inch inside under renovation into condominiums that will look out onto Courthouse Square.

Tourism is the new main industry. Every summer, the town

celebrates Stage Coach Days; every fall, the Fire Ant Festival. Every Christmas, the people decorate the historic buildings for the Wonderland of Lights Festival. Texas clay is perfect for pottery, and Marshall has been manufacturing stoneware for over a century. Today, thirteen local plants and five outlet stores give the city claim to the title of Pottery Capital of the United States.

Some of downtown Marshall hasn't changed all that much, physically, that is, since Joe lived there. A stately telephone company building built a year before Joe was born is still there, and the first floor is now the Michelson Museum of Art, dedicated to the work of Russian-American artist Leo Michelson and to traveling exhibits. Nearby, the Paramount Theatre, where Joe and other Marshall Blacks had to use the back door and sit in the balcony, stands empty. The marquee that once announced the movies Joe saw for a dime, when he had one, now says ISTORIC A MOSPHE IC THEATRE FOR SALE, with a phone number.

Some of the old buildings on this square have been restored by the city or the county. Many storefronts are empty. At lunchtime on a sunny weekday you can stand for minutes on the brick-paved street without needing to move for a passing car.

In what used to be the First National Bank on the square, a Mexican restaurant is bustling at lunchtime. You can still make out the old outlines of the offices and the teller window, but now the place serves hot food and cold beer. The customers are Black, White and Mexican. Joe came in here one day many years ago to repay a man a dollar and change. The bank staff told him to get out. Today Joe gets a combination plate and asks the waitress for a side salad. "Yes, sir," she says, smiling. He doesn't take this for granted. Hardly any of the restaurants that were here when Joe was a boy served Blacks. To buy a hamburger for ten cents, Joe had to stand outside the window and hold up a finger. Then he'd have to go to the back door and have it handed out to him in a paper bag.

Many of the old houses west of the main square still look grand even while standing empty. The little brick building that was Ice Company #2 sits on a corner near Marshall High, permanently closed with a faded OPEN sign in the window. The jewelry shop where Horace Massengale worked is now part of a furniture store on East Austin. Horace was Hugh Massengale's eldest son, the older brother Joe never knew.

A feed mill looms over the Marshall Cemetery on Grand Avenue, where new marble headstones mark the graves of soldiers from the Confederate States of America who died in local hospitals during the Civil War. A few have names: "Jonathan Adams, Baird's Reg't., Texas Cav, CSA, June 15, 1865." Most are unknown. They lie with General Walter Paye Lane and other prominent Confederate soldiers and officials. All are remembered with tiny flags, the Stars and Bars under which they fought. An obelisk was erected to them in tribute by the United Daughters of the Confederacy, and it still stands in the corner by Repose and Columbus Streets.

One Amtrak train going east and one going west leave the old Texas and Pacific depot every day, now restored in the Ginocchio Historic District. The gentleman working in the museum inside has time to talk about the days when these tracks carried soldiers to war and cotton to market.

Pemberton High School, Joe's alma mater, still stands, but the name lives on only among its graduates. It was merged with Marshall High School in 1970. Wiley College thrives in its second century. A promo for the station recorded by Joe, still a disk jockey at heart, plays all the time on the college radio station.

The old shops along Marshall's downtown streets compete today against the Wal-Mart Supercenter two miles outside the old city. Most of the business traffic runs along Route 59, where the newer hotels, shops and restaurants all line up like hitchhikers trying to get to Dallas. The center of Marshall is dark and deserted at night. White lights high in the windows of the shell of the Hotel Marshall spell DREAM BIG.

ONE TOURIST went back to Marshall in the spring of 2005. Joe Massengale was home to visit the old places so that he could tell his story here.

Different as the city looks, the countryside outside Marshall is very little changed from the days when Hugh and Susie Massengale lived there. Some of the roads have been paved, but the red clay underneath comes up through the cracks in the asphalt when it rains. In springtime, the woods and fields bloom with daffodils in yellow bunches, azaleas, white and purple irises, dogwoods. Hawks and buzzards circle overhead, watching for rabbits and squirrels. The pines grow straight a hundred fifty feet tall on the same land Hugh Massengale worked.

Joe's birthplace is marked by a huge vine-covered oak tree

that was there at the time, but not a trace of the building can be seen on the overgrown lot. Joe walks into the brush looking for it. "Best I can tell is that the house was right back up in here somewhere," he says. "That might be where it was. I know that old tree. That was it. I'm surprised I can find the place at all." He walks along the rutted path off a narrow logging road, peering into the woods. This was the place that burned, where his father tossed him out the window wrapped in a straw mattress. "This is it, right here," he says, his feet crunching through the brush. Someone recently used the spot to dump trash. An old couch and rusty barrels lie there. A realtor's FOR SALE sign sticks up from the heap.

The house Hugh found empty at Hezzie Cook Road and FM 1186, the one where he read the Sunday paper to gathered neighbors, is long gone. Not even a chimney foundation remains.

The addresses of Joe's old neighbors are still there, but the houses on those lots are new. Many of them are double-wide prefabs. Others are handsome new brick with big satellite antennas in the yards and boats in the driveway to take to nearby Caddo Lake. Some people keep longhorn cattle and even camels penned behind their houses.

The field where Joe held his end of a two-man saw and decided never again to get thrown out of school is still open land. The Sabine River, where he and his brothers swam, and the fields he plowed when he was providing for his family, look just as they did during the 1930s.

The WPA-built Community Center where Joe heard his father sing is long since abandoned, but parts of the buildings still stand, the log walls and chimneys still braced there against the East Texas wind that turns into a tornado before you know it. The baseball field out back where Blacks and Whites played and sat separately is a yard high with weeds and flowers, and the sound here now is the song of mockingbirds. All around are hay farms, corn fields, open pastures with horses or Angus cattle; small houses, oil rigs and gas wells, and quiet.

Joe's cousins would never forgive him if he didn't stop by, and he visits them all for hours on this trip. Many of the people he knew as a boy still live on the land their families worked, now in handsome new houses with green lawns. Hugh Massengale's name is still spoken respectfully by the ones who remember how hard he worked. They call him "Mister Hugh," and they want to know how the kid who wore women's shoes to school back then is doing in Los Angeles. Joe has a standing offer of five acres of his cousins' old holdings to build himself a house if he ever wants to come back.

It takes minutes to drive by George Foreman's huge ranch. Foreman's pinto ponies and ostriches wander in a big open field by a pond near the road where Joe saw Bakey Makum killed. All the neighbors know when Foreman is home. He ran these roads when he trained to fight. He still likes to walk them and talk with people.

Hugh Massengale lies in a tiny cemetery near a Baptist church. His marker is inscribed "Asleep in Jesus," with the dates of his life, and has the compass-and-square insignia of a Freemason. Many Brookses and Waltons from Susie Massengale's side of the family lie here. There are fresh flowers on some of the graves, but few new markers. Some of the old ones are homemade with cement, with the name of the loved one written with a twig.

▦

EIGHT OF the remaining members of Marshall's Pemberton High School Class of 1947 join Joe for lunch at a restaurant downtown in J. Weisman and Co. Department Store. It was renovated by the city during the 1990s, and today it's an artists' cooperative that sells local crafts and serves great food.

These are old friends, some Joe hasn't seen for sixty years. Some left and came back, some stayed all this time to watch Marshall transform. They include a former mayor of the city, schoolteachers and businesswomen and the friend from whom Joe borrowed a suit in 1947 to go to the senior prom.

They say grace thanking God for the food, for the fellowship and "for the brother among us who has come home to his roots."

They bring envelopes of old memorabilia, class programs, photos and a few funeral programs, and pass them around as they share iced tea and chicken salad, catching up with the kids and grandchildren and great-grandchildren all over the world.

They talk about staying busy, substitute teaching, gardening, traveling, laughing in voices sweetened by many years and many memories. They remember the teachers who held them to demanding standards. Professor Pemberton would examine them all in the morning and make them go home if they weren't presentable for school, regardless of how far they'd come to get there, or of whether they'd walked five miles or taken their last bath cold in a steel washtub. It helped make them all strong.

The children of the people gathered at this table are like Joe's sons, business executives, doctors, teachers, men and women in uniform serving their country abroad or at sea. Some of them have never seen Marshall, but like the Massengales, their stories began here.

Joe and his friends honor the past by meeting this way, but the present and the future are where their attention lies. As their reminiscences are shared, it becomes clear that Joe Massengale's story is not unique at all, and not even unusual in a thousand places like Marshall. All of them around this table struggled against the same intolerance. The best story of this gathering is the most obvious one. When they were students together, they would not have been allowed to come here and have lunch. Today they can take it for granted. The family histories that started here might all have ended as abruptly as Joe's history nearly did that day in the Square when the townsmen were ready to kill Hugh Massengale. Instead, only the early chapters have been written. Joe and his friends worked all their lives for something so fine and simple as this.

They say another prayer and part with a chorus from the old school song, "Pemberton Forever."

IN THE heart of Joe Massengale's hometown, the Harrison County Courthouse sits in the same broad brick-paved plaza that was there when Joe was a boy. As Joe visits this time, the building is being restored inside and out. Joe's Hall of Fame memorabilia are in storage.

Surrounded by a chain-link construction fence, the Courthouse glows. The golden brick and pink granite have been scrubbed clean. The inside is stripped to the walls and wiring. Sounds of saws and drills echo from within. The cornerstone of the building, laid in 1905, bears the same compass-and-square Masonic symbol that is carved on Hugh Massengale's gravestone.

"Rock of Ages" chimes from First Methodist Church as Joe walks around the Courthouse. The pecan trees around the building are wrapped in thousands of lights.

"I walked through here many a day," Joe says. "I shined shoes right here. I used to bring my shine box to school with me and come over here after I got off school at Pemberton High. Five cents a shine. Often as not, they'd run kids like me off." Right here, when he was living in his first apartment in town for three dollars a month and working at the café at the bus station, Joe saw his father in the square and gave Hugh a dollar. It still makes Joe proud to remember the smile on Hugh's face, and his father's voice saying, "Thank you, Joe, you're doing all right."

You don't know until you stand there that the spot where Hugh Massengale nearly died was within a short walk of three churches. The spires of Trinity Episcopal Church and First Baptist Church are still visible to the west, and the American eagle looks down from the pediment of the west front of the Courthouse on the place where the men held him and debated Hugh's fate as Joe watched.

ON THE other side of the Courthouse stands the statue of the young Confederate soldier. The elegy on the south side of the statue's pedestal seems to promise that the old spirit of separation lingers:

> *And by God's help while our heart shall live*
> *It shall keep in its faithful way*
> *The camp-fires lit for the men in gray . . .*

But on the north side is carved a gentler note of reconciliation.

> *No more they hear the rebel yell*
> *Where battle thunders rose and fell*
> *'Tis now a welcome and a cheer*
> *To friends, to foemen, far and near*
> *And peace, sweet peace, born of despair*
> *Walks forth and sheds her radiance fair*
> *Upon lost fields of honor.*

It was to soldiers like this, men very uncertain of their futures, men still eager to carry on the cause, that Robert E. Lee spoke after the surrender of the Army of Northern Virginia at Appomattox. The story is told that many of Lee's men wanted to ignore the surrender and continue the fight. Lee told them no. He asked them to invest themselves in a future that was better, and to hope that those to come would build communities where the old fears and furies would find no home. The general gave them the very lesson Joe Massengale took from Marshall and used to build his family: "Abandon your animosities," Lee told his men, "and make your sons Americans."

AND FROM this place began new stories and old lessons being taught today by the six Massengale sons all over the United States.

At the James Rhoads School at 50th and North Parrish in West Philadelphia, all the teachers wear *Cat in the Hat* hats as part of the Philadelphia Reads! Program. The cinderblock walls in the classrooms are brightened by posters, drawings and valentines for the teachers.

Joe Massengale, Jr., wears casual clothes sometimes to show a house to prospective buyers, but for visits to the school he always wears a jacket and tie.

As a volunteer today, Joe Jr. sits one-by-one with the kids at their tables and asks them to read to him from books on the Arctic, on animals, hurricanes and Dr. Seuss. Some of the kids aren't used to reading aloud and they whisper in his ear as his finger follows the lines word by word.

He knows all their names and makes sure to use them. He encourages them all with questions, cajoling and open affection: "Tell Mister Joe something good!" He asks about what they do at home, about their plans, about college. He sits with one boy who wants to be a football player. Joe Jr. emphasizes academics as a way into athletics, talking about college ball and about how smart good players need to be. "Grades are the key—you can't play if you can't get good grades," he tells the boy. "I know you can do it."

He asks for confidence from all of them. "Show it to me," he says. "When I walk in, I want to see some commitment." And he praises every effort. "Man, I'm going to tell you something—you're doing a great job and I really appreciate it."

School officials in Philadelphia estimate that about 45 percent of children in the city's educational system do not read at grade level by fourth grade. Most do not attend preschool. Four out of five students belong to families who may not have any books at all at home. Many of these kids may not ever have been read to, or have read to anyone. And almost nine out of ten children who appear in the city's juvenile court lack basic reading skills.

Joe Jr. calls these children "my kids."

The teachers love seeing him. There are few men at Rhoads, and few come in from the community to help. He is a personal friend and resource for the staff as well as for the students. They consult with him about tough cases, or just lean on him a little for support.

This is the only place besides church where Joe turns the ringer on his cell phone off. "My job," he says, "is to get these kids to know they're loved and respected," and he doesn't let the telephone interrupt. It buzzes again and again in his pocket while he talks with the kids until one of them finally laughs out loud, "Mister Joe's gonna blow up!"

At home in his office is a framed poem written to Joe Jr. from a friend at church, which reads in part,

On your 50th Birthday I wish for you a return on your investment

In the lives of so many people, who through you have received a blessing

May each day God entrusts to you bring much joy and gladness of heart

Because of you my life has been blessed; thank you for playing a part.

MICHAEL MASSENGALE continues to coach actors in one of the most adverse job markets the entertainment business has ever experienced. Reality television, computer animation and high production costs have changed the labor economics of movies and TV, forcing many working actors to take less money or leave the business. Young actors still want to try.

"The key lesson to understand right now," Michael says at home in Los Angeles, "is that with more competition than ever for fewer roles, you need to stand out. You cannot call yourself an actor if I can barely hear you talk. We just held auditions for *North on South Central*. I told the new ones, 'If you're going to be wrong, be LOUD and wrong. You can't stand up there and be fearful. Be *strong*. Be decisive, be present. It's not just about acting; it's about your life. You need to *declare*. Let me know you stand out more than the next one who comes in. You need to do it before you say a word. Throw those shoulders back, hold your head up, stand up here and say with conviction who you are and what you want. Project!'

"They're inexperienced, and so they're nervous," he continues. "But we're in the toughest market I ever saw, and so they'd better show some fortitude from the time they commit to it. They'd better be adaptable for anything that gets tossed at them, and hungry for every part. Some of these kids are terrified, but I tell them, 'If it's your passion, respect that passion. Embrace it. Be ready to support yourself any way you can.'

"I'm in the same situation myself. I just went on an audition for a cop drama. I was in there competing with people who are a lot younger than I am. I didn't get the part, but the producers liked the way I read, and they'll call me back for something else. That's happening a lot lately. The casting director tells me they want to build something for me to do that's bigger than the role they had me reading for.

"I'm stretching myself as an actor further than I ever did. Many of the actors I know, if they're having any success, are staying in their niche because the business is so tough right now. If they have a steady gig with commercials or stage they're not looking for anything that would jeopardize that. Personally, I don't think you can play it safe. There's no real security in that anyway. You have to keep trying.

"Remember the young guy who played the kid at the bus stop in *North on South Central*? He comes by my house before he auditions. We work on the roles he's up for, on keeping his concentration. We all lose that single-mindedness sometimes, and I have to ask, 'Hey, man, are you *here*?' He just landed a three-picture deal. The day he heard about it, he'd bought a suit to go on a job interview with Federal Express. He thought he was out of acting. His manager called and told him he made it. I let him know how proud of him I was."

Michael's encouragement goes to the kids in the neighborhood as well as to his professional colleagues. The frame of his kitchen door is marked with pencil lines and written names and dates showing their respective heights. Michael and his wife make them welcome. They go to the children's grade-school graduation ceremonies and to their high school basketball games. "I appreciate that the parents let me in their kids' lives. It means a lot to me to help these kids get a sense of being somebody."

LARRY MASSENGALE, driving home in Los Angeles from his last job of the day, says he finds it hard sometimes to get the help he needs to keep up with business. "I hire younger guys for my crew when I can get them, but it's tough finding the work ethic I need to keep the standards I want. They're good guys, but the energy isn't always there. They want to get paid and be on their way. I worry that they're missing the point. They don't take the same pride in it that I do. The rewards for me are the relationships I have with my clients, their trust. Look at what I do . . . anyone can wash a car. Plenty of guys do it this well. But I don't think they get as much back from it as I get. The regard of my clients, their trust, their goodwill and friendship; the work is secondary to the attitude I give and get back. That's the real payment.

"My father used to invest himself that way in his landscaping work. That perfectionism—it didn't always make sense if you look at it just from the point of view of money. The clients just as likely would have been happy with work that wasn't that good. They'd have paid him for that happily. But he said, no, this isn't just about the money. It was about the personal reward he got out of doing a good job. He needed to impress himself as much as he needed to impress anyone else; more, really, when I think about it, because the clients hardly ever knew that this guy in coveralls working on their yards owned horses and drove a Rolls and all that. He never tried to impress anyone with what he had. But what he *did*, how he worked: that was everything, and he gave that all he had, all the time. That was how he invested, and how he made progress. That was how he earned what he got. He took an inch forward at a time, not overreaching, not making imprudent choices, and he never retreated. He made mistakes and he took his losses but he never doubted himself.

"He knew who he was. He chose his fights and chose carefully. You have to pick your fights, and I know that from the mistakes I made myself. When I was younger I wanted everything at once, and I was just going to bang my head against the wall until I got it. I found out that that wall is a lot thicker than my head. Try to bulldoze it down and you get nowhere. Let anger or arrogance take you over and you'll end up with nothing. This has nothing to do with the color of your skin. It has everything to do with life, with the choices anybody makes. *The Art of War* by Sun Tzu says it: Don't squander yourself in the wrong places. Invest carefully, with patience, with faith in who you are, and you win."

"THE THING I enjoy so much about my dad and his career," Randy Massengale says, "was that he didn't know day-to-day what would happen, but he still trusted his ability to succeed without a safety net. He was like a tightrope walker crossing on sheer skill. He didn't worry about tomorrow. He was completely focused on getting it right today, on this job, right now, and being judged for it. He didn't make the mistake many people feel they need to make, of trading in his creativity and versatility for the sake of security and cash flow."

As his team makes final preparations for their trip overseas, and his company stands on the brink of realizing all he's worked for since he started it, Randy considers the risk he's taking with Spinoza, and what he aims to get in return.

"Everyone has a personal investment strategy," he says. "It's the habits and expectations and assumptions that guide you every day, whether or not you know it. Money happens when you invest yourself wisely. You can blow it, you can get more, but you can't get yesterday back. It's much more important than money how you utilize your time, and people who are successful know that today is precious. That's the biggest pressure I feel, to use the time I have.

"I always ask my students, 'Do you want to be a catalyst, or the beneficiary of an effort?' What they say tells me a lot about them. The ones who want to be catalysts take pleasure in the effort it takes to make a success. They like the work. The rewards aren't on their minds. They're risk-takers.

"That's its own reward. If you do that you never need to apologize for what you get in life. You've earned it in the right way. The wealth we inherited from my dad can never be lost or taken away from us because it wasn't money. It was character. We've taken what he gave us and invested it our whole lives.

"Every class I teach, I meet students who think they know what success looks like. House, car, big office, big title, all that, and nobody has challenged their thinking on what it really takes to be successful. They're looking for security by any immediate means they can get, instead of investing themselves in real work. They're daunted by the effort it takes to build something. Instead of seeing it for the valuable uphill climb it is, they despair about the effort it takes and the time that goes into it.

"But those things are the point. The real value is the challenges you undertake, not what you get afterwards in terms of reward.

"Right now there are eleven Massengale grandkids. My brothers and I are asking ourselves how these lessons we learned from our Dad will be learned by the next generation. We wonder if by making it easier for the next ones, if we're really helping them. Like all parents we want our kids to have things we didn't have, lessons and training and education for the things they want to pursue, but still . . . sometimes I feel that the best thing I can do for my kids is to say no. No lessons, no theory. If you want to learn how to be an athlete, *play*. If you want to learn to be a singer, *sing*. Jump in the deep end and learn as fast as you can. Trial and error is painful. But, man, you keep what it teaches you. And above all, *persist*, and use what you learn.

"I went to South Africa for Microsoft before the formal ending of apartheid, and it was like nothing I'd ever experienced. Just *being*, just being alive, was a virtual death sentence for millions of people back then. I felt in a small way that my being there, a Black executive doing business, was part of dismantling that kind of oppression. Apartheid was anathema to the human condition, and I felt honored that I could do my part in helping them join the twenty-first century, where attitudes like that should have no place, any more than they should have had when my father was a boy in Texas.

"Horace Mann said: 'Be ashamed to die until you have won some victory for humanity.' That one little victory was enough for me. My dad's life is his victory in the same way. He lasted longer than the things he fought against, the things that fought him. He applied the best parts of himself, and he won."

IN HIS spare time, whether he has any or not, Patrick Massengale coaches a youth league basketball team in Denver. The kids are White, Black and Latino like the changing Colorado population. Pat sweats and suffers through every miss and lapse a twelve-year-old can make, and he's equally gruff and equally loving with them all, his own kids and the ones on the other team too. It's about teamwork for him. He'd rather the boys lose well as a team than win by hotdogging and selfishness. When he huddles the boys to give them direction, they break up with a chant: "ONETWOTHREE SACRIFICE!"

He keeps his brothers posted by e-mail about the team's fortunes.

Subject: Brothas!
Man

    The season is over, but what a roller-coaster ride.
    On Sunday we played two games and split them. We

lost the first one to some military kids from Colorado Springs. A very disciplined team. They did not show any emotion, just execution. Good kids, but they played like a machine. I hope they were having some fun.

Their coach stayed around to watch our next game against Lutheran (11-3). They were the favorite in our level of the competition. Our kids jumped right on them. I put a faster, smaller lineup than usual on the floor to start. I thought my kids were finally ready to rely on athletics to win a game.

We ran Lutheran down pretty well with the starters. Then I sent some bruisers in to soften them up. So . . . seconds left in the first half. We're up by five. I tell my kids to cover the floor and spread out to use up the time on the clock. I knew if we were shooting, Lutheran would get the rebounds and come back, no matter how little time there was left on the clock.

All of my kids' parents yell from the stands, "Shoot! Shoot! Shoot!" to their boys. Guess what? Our guys gun one. Lutheran gets the rebound, hits the jumper and draws a foul. We're down by two.

We lose the ball on a turnover. They shoot again and tie it up going into the half.

I pleaded with my guys, "Just for the day, just for the next fifteen minutes, don't listen to your parents when they tell you to shoot for yourself. Play for the team, not for the points. Get the best shot, even if it isn't your shot."

They ran that half beautifully. We stayed ahead on speed and execution, though they had us on height and strength. We were up by two as the clock wound down.

End of the fourth quarter. I put a kid in to just help our guys run off eight seconds for the win, and his parents yell, "Shoot!" Boom, he shoots a brick. Lutheran rebounds, puts one up. Tie score.

Overtime. My guys draw fouls from their big man and he's out of the game. Nobody scores for minutes, and then I tell my kids to run our pick-and-roll. It works. We're up by two. Then Lutheran sinks one from the corner.

Tie. Double overtime. Sudden death.

Right off we foul them. One free throw and it's over. They miss two. We get the rebound, run the length of the floor for a lay-up . . . and miss. I call time out, grab the kid who missed and just kiss him on his forehead and hug him, I felt so bad for him.

I knew it couldn't end like this. My stepson fires the ball down the floor to a kid who gets the pass underneath and bang, lay-up. Game over.

Parents scream. Kids jump off the bench. Lutheran is crushed. I go to each kid on Lutheran's team and hug and kiss them all. I hug their coaches.

Then I pull my team aside and address my guys . . . what a game! For the second week in a row, my kids knock off the favorite.

We wait around for twenty-four hours to see if we make it to the next round, and we were denied. The kids were very upset. I can say there were at least two teams out there who felt we were the toughest team they played all season. My guys are looking forward to next year. This one taught them the most important lessons: be fearless; stick together; win for the team and you win for yourself.

It was fun, and all of the kids got better, and that was what counted. God is good! I love y'all, kiss your families for us and thank you for everything.

ANDRE MASSENGALE started his first full-time job in March 2005. A social services agency in Los Angeles placed him with a nationally known toy company. Joe's Expert Tree Service is finally winding down as the founder approaches his ninth decade, so the youngest of the Massengale brothers joins the rest in making his own way.

Andre has what he needs. The lessons Joe taught him about listening, focusing and confidence in himself all run deep in his character.

"I leave the house at 7:15," Andre says. "I take the freeway to get to work by 8:30. They gave me a few days' training, and soon it was all familiar to me.

"I'm a good person and I want to do everything right. The things my dad showed me about being honest and focused, about looking neat and being pleasant to people . . . that's what I know how to do. He trained me in everything.

"I'm one of the youngest people there. I work with other people on the crew. We all help each other out.

"It feels good to be independent. I still go to my dad's house every weekend, and help him with the yard or with things like putting up the Christmas lights. I worry sometimes about him, because I don't want him to be alone, but he knows I'm here if he needs me. And I know I can get along in my life now. He gave me that. I know I can take care of myself."

By the end of his first pay period, Andre earned a raise.

"THEY SAY you can't go home again," Joe says. "But you can. You have to. Truth is, you never really leave."

He walks around the Courthouse in his hometown by the markers commemorating the scientists and business leaders, the artists and the soldiers from Marshall who made their marks on the world.

"I learned a lot after I left here. I learned about the tree business and about the music business and about Thorough-bred racing. I learned about raising a family and about own-ing a home. But the lessons I learned here were the start of all that. I moved away from here but I kept my Marshall raising. And I wouldn't give it up for anything."

It's a little hard for him to talk about all this. Seventy-six years of memories come back to Joe at this place where so much happened to him. He has to pause a moment.

"Growing up here . . . it taught me how to be a man. There were times when people tried to tell me, and everyone like me, that we couldn't be men, but *I am a man*. I know I am. That's the message of my whole life. And for every time people tried to take that away from me, there was someone else in my life who made sure I never forgot it, and that I lived up to what it means.

"My father saw the strength in me and my brothers and sis-ters. He wouldn't let us see ourselves any other way, just as he never permitted himself to feel weak or helpless. When there was nothing else to live on but character, that's what kept him going. He made sure it was the same for me.

"My teachers at Pemberton High School, the ministers in church: they all went through the same things I did, and worse. They understood. Their messages were the same. Even if you have nothing, you have no excuses. Find the faith in yourself, find the strength. Do the work anyway. Bitterness and helplessness get you nowhere. And look, in this country there's a way for people who give the best of themselves. There's always a way. They believed that. They made me believe it too.

"Man, that was love. All that discipline was, was love. It gave me what I needed to stay alive, to walk a straight road and know that the future would be better if I did my part. It was true. It was always true.

"People back here would stay in touch with us in Los Angeles, so we were never really far from home. The Marshall folks would ask, 'What's Joe doing now?' He's in the family business, he's on the radio, he's racing horses. I was proud that they knew I was making progress. I wasn't going to come to Los Angeles and be a fool. My teachers, my ministers, my brothers, they set a standard for me, just as my father did, and I wanted to live up to that. They took responsibility. I wanted to repay them for that."

Drills and saws whine from within the Courthouse. When the building is finished inside, the plaza outside will be refurbished with new brick paving and landscaping. Joe looks around at all the buildings being saved as Marshall rebuilds.

"Some of what I learned here seems missing from people's lives today, and it needs to be talked about and faced. I see young people dying in Los Angeles. Every night on the news, young men leaving school, leaving children behind. Dropping out of school with no skills at all, no place to go. Kids grow up not knowing their fathers, not knowing how to live. People shooting each other on the streets. Boys killing boys. So many lives just wasted. People giving up on themselves, losing hope. It shouldn't be that way.

"I look at the anger I see there, the violence, and I wonder why people still don't seek something better from themselves and each other. I know things can change. They changed right here. People right here in Marshall lived that change. They all saw a better way. They made it happen. Look around the table today at lunch. You'd never have believed that would ever happen sixty years ago. That's a miracle. A miracle. I know my grandchildren might never understand how things like I saw here ever happened. But they'll have their own situations to face, and maybe my example will show them that they have the same strength to do what they want to do in life.

"Things change when we change them. It starts right here. That's what people need to believe."

▓

A SPECIAL commission from Harrison County, the City of Marshall, the Historical Museum, the Chamber of Commerce and the County Historical Commission is directing this effort to save the Courthouse where Joe's path in life came so close to changing that day seventy years ago when his father Hugh was almost taken from him.

When construction began, the commission reached out to people all over the country to seek contributions for a long and costly effort that now shows the first signs of success to come. People were invited to purchase bricks for new paving around the Courthouse. Thirty-five dollars will buy a brick, standard size, with a name inscribed on it. That brick will become part of the new walkway around the building.

Joe donated one for every member of his family. When asked why, he says simply, "They asked me."

He continues: "They gave me a place in the Hall of Fame in this building. And you may not find ten Black families who have their names here. People remember the bad things. I think differently about that, I guess. I thought I owed my family something about remembering the good. My grandchildren will come here to see these names after I'm gone. I hope they'll think about what their ancestors did, what I did. I hope they'll see the good too.

"There's so much I might have taken away from here, but a man has to ask himself what to keep and what to let go. I had anger and I had bad memories. And I had things I knew were precious. I had my family's love and my teachers' faith. I had what I learned from my father about work and discipline. I had to make something good from those things. You have to make something happen. That's the only way things change. It was my life, it was my opportunity. The ones who cared for me had watched out for me and they weren't going to let me waste it. They believed in me. Sometimes when your will fails you, it's other people's belief in you that keeps you going. It was the good things like that, the hopeful things, that mattered. That's what I kept.

"The lessons I got right here are the ones that I used my whole life. They're the same ones I taught my sons. Stay strong, never lose faith, keep your priorities straight and never give up. That's why I come back. That's why this is still home."

On the new foundation Joe and his family have built around the country, the next generation of Massengales will create lives and careers that their forebears might barely have dreamed possible. And here where the family story began, the work on the Courthouse is heading toward completion. When the building and the plaza are done, the names of all the members of Joe Massengale's family will forever be part of the heart of Marshall. The place where Hugh was spared, but where he could not be called a man, will bear his name, and the name of Susie Massengale, and the names of Joe's brothers and sisters, Bob, Alzie, Fred, Herbert, Oliver, Olivia, Ollie, Alfred, Lendell, Idell, Willie Ruth, and the little brother who did not live long enough to have a name of his own. Lady Justice and the eagles on the Courthouse will overlook the spot, and this little part of America will be restored.

Miracle things happen.

Joe smiles as he thinks of it. "It's something what a man goes through in a lifetime, isn't it?"

SOURCES

The authors wish to acknowledge the following sources and interviews:

Edward R. Ritvo, M.D., What You ~~Should~~ Must Know About Autism and Asperger's Syndrome. Unpublished manuscript, 2004.

Ted Gioia, *West Coast Jazz: Modern Jazz in California 1945–1960*. New York: Oxford University Press. 1992.

Clora Bryant, et al., eds., *Central Avenue Sounds. Jazz in Los Angeles*. Los Angeles: University of California Press. 1998.

John D. Thomas, "Black in the Saddle: The Great African-American Jockeys Are Riding Back into History." *Village Voice*, February 10–16, 1999.

Leslie Walker, "The Unknown Hunting for Renown." *The Washington Post*, February 17, 2005, page E01.

John O'Neil, "Slow-Motion Miracle: One Boy's Journey Out of Autism's Grasp." *New York Times*, December 29, 2004;

Anahad O'Connor, "In Autism, New Goal Is Finding It Soon Enough to Fight It." *New York Times*, December 14, 2004.

Anthony Walton, "Technology Versus African-Americans." *The Atlantic Monthly*, January 1999, v283 i1 p14(1).

Julia Angwin and Laura Castaneda, "The Digital Divide High-Tech Boom a Bust for Blacks, Latinos." *San Francisco Chronicle*, May 4, 1998.

Nathaniel "Magnificent" Montague with Bob Baker. *Burn, Baby! Burn! The Autobiography of Magnificent Montague*. Chicago: University of Illinois Press, 2003.

Interview with R. Wayne Hicks, President, Black Data Processing Association, December 15, 2004.

Interview with Laurie Stephens, Ph.D., Director, Autism Spectrum Disorders Programs, Young Learners and Village Glen, The Help Group, Los Angeles, CA, March 21, 2005.

ABOUT THE CONTRIBUTORS

DENNIS C. RICHMOND, SR.

Joe Massengale and his six sons *(left to right)*:
Michael, Joe, Larry, Andre, Patrick, Randy and Joe Jr.

The Sons

JOSEPH MASSENGALE, JR., is the principal of Spirit Financial Group of Wynnewood, Pennsylvania.

MICHAEL MASSENGALE is an actor and real estate broker in Los Angeles. His acting credits include films such as Mark Brown's *Two Can Play That Game*, Robert Altman's *The Long Goodbye*, and Christian du Lac's *Mr. Millennium*, among others. He has appeared onstage as Lenny in Steinbeck's *Of Mice and Men*, George Murchison in *A Raisin in the Sun*, and Old Willie in *North on South Central Avenue* as well as in numerous local and national television commercials.

LAWRENCE MASSENGALE owns Complete Auto Detailing in Encino, California.

RANDY MASSENGALE is the founder and CEO of Spinoza Technology, Inc., and has worked in leading technology companies for over thirty years. He is the founder of The Cherubs, a Seattle-based venture capital group dedicated to funding early-stage companies involved with disruptive technologies, and serves on the board of regents at Seattle University and on the board of trustees at Lewis & Clark College in Portland.

PATRICK MASSENGALE runs two companies, a car and airplane cleaning business and a mobile catering company, in the Denver area.

ANDRE MASSENGALE was the last of Joe's sons to grow up in the family business. He works today with a Los Angeles toy company.

Contributors

GEORGE FOREMAN, Olympic heavyweight boxing champion in 1968 and two-time heavyweight boxing champion of the world, is founder of the George Foreman Youth and Community Center, and the author of two autobiographical bestsellers, *By George: The Autobiography of George Foreman* and *George Foreman's Guide to Life,* and two popular barbecue cookbooks. An ordained minister, he started his ministry after a religious experience that took place in his dressing room after he lost to Jimmy Young in 1977. He spreads the Gospel at The Church of Lord Jesus Christ in Houston. The father of ten children, he lives with his family in Texas.

GUY BLUFORD, JR., PH.D., spent fifteen years with NASA as one of its elite astronauts. A member of the first class of space shuttle astronauts, in 1983 he became the first African-American to fly in space. He also flew on a Spacelab flight in 1985 and on Department of Defense missions in 1991 and 1992. Upon his retirement from NASA in 1993, he had logged over 688 hours in space. He was inducted into the International Space Hall of Fame in 1997.

A former fighter pilot in Vietnam, he served twenty-nine years in the United States Air Force as a tactical fighter pilot, instructor pilot, staff development engineer and Branch Chief of the Aerodynamics and Airframe Branch of the Air Force Flight Dynamics Laboratory. He has over 5,200 hours of jet flight time in ten different aircraft. Today Dr. Bluford serves as President of the Aerospace Technology Group (ATG), an aerospace technology and business consulting organization.

A native of Philadelphia, Dr. Bluford holds bachelor's, master's and doctorate degrees in aerospace engineering, as well as a master's of business administration. He has earned thirteen honorary doctorate degrees and he conducts a very active civic life.

ANJELICA HUSTON is an Academy Award–winning actress and critically acclaimed director. Huston received the Best Supporting Actress Oscar for her role as Maerose Prizzi in *Prizzi's Honor*, for which she also won the Los Angeles and New York Film Critics Awards. The film was her first adult collaboration with her father, director, writer and actor John Huston, who himself won Oscars for Best Director and Best Screenplay in 1948 for *The Treasure of the Sierra Madre*—the film for which her grandfather, Walter Huston, won the Best Supporting Actor Oscar. She earned additional Academy Award nominations for her roles in *Enemies: A Love Story* and *The Grifters*, and won critical acclaim for her performances in *The Royal Tenenbaums; The Addams Family* and *Addams Family Values; The Witches;* and *Ever After*, for which she won the Block-buster Entertainment Award for Best Supporting Actress; *The Crossing Guard*, for which she received a Golden Globe nomination for Best Supporting Actress; *Daddy Day Care;* Clint

Eastwood's *Blood Work;* Woody Allen's *Manhattan Murder Mystery* and *Crimes and Misdemeanors*; *Gardens of Stone*; *Buffalo '66*; *The Golden Bowl*; *A Handful of Dust*; *Mr. North*; *The Perez Family* and her father's last film, *The Dead.* Her most recent projects include Wes Anderson's *The Life Aquatic with Steve Zissou* and Terry Zwigoff's *Art School Confidential.*

In television, she received an Emmy nomination for Best Supporting Actress, as well as a SAG Award nomination, for the miniseries *The Mists of Avalon;* for her performances in the mini-series *Buffalo Girls* and *Lonesome Dove*; and for her work in HBO's *Iron Jawed Angels.* She was nominated for a Golden Globe Award for her performance in the television film *Family Pictures.*

Huston made her directorial debut in 1996 with her unflinching adaptation of the best-seller *Bastard Out of Carolina,* for which she was nominated for both a Director's Guild of America Award and an Emmy from the Academy of Television Arts & Sciences. She directed, produced and starred in *Agnes Browne,* and directed Rosie O'Donnell and Andie MacDowell in the Hallmark/CBS television movie *Riding the Bus with My Sister.*

RAFER JOHNSON won the gold medal in the decathlon for the United States in the 1960 Olympics in Rome. He is a three-time world record holder in the event and a silver medalist at the 1956 Olympics. He went on to a successful career in business and public service, helping numerous humanitarian and medical organizations throughout the country.

In 1969, Johnson helped to found California Special Olympics to inspire and serve individuals with mental retardation.

For four decades, CSO has been a principal focus of Rafer's life, along with family. He was elected president and served in that capacity until July 1992, when he was named Chairman of the Board of Governors. From the original competition involving 900 athletes, Rafer has led the growth of Special Olympics' Southern California organization to more than 11,000 children and adults with intellectual disabilities in Southern California. As he stated in an interview in the UCLA monthly, "I've just always felt that I owed something back to my state, my community and to young people. I'm not sure that I'll ever feel like I've repaid the debt. I think I'll always feel some obligation because I received so much." He has served on behalf of numerous humanitarian organizations, all aimed at helping young people and communities to grow, experience new opportunities, and "be the best that they can be."

KENT DESORMEAUX was sixteen when he rode his first winning Thoroughbred. By twenty-seven, he was the youngest jockey to surpass $100 million in career purses. He won his first Eclipse Award in 1987 as the year's top apprentice jockey, and two more as a journeyman in 1989 and 1992. In 1989, Kent surpassed the record for victories in a year by riding 598 winners, breaking Chris McCarron's 1974 record of 546, becoming one of three jockeys to lead the nation in wins three consecutive years.

In 1992, he sustained a major head injury, but he returned the next year to win his first Breeders' Cup aboard Kotashaan in the Turf. Kotashaan would go on to Horse of the Year honors that year. Also in 1993, Kent received the George Woolf Award. The Woolf Award honors riders whose careers and personal character reflect positively on themselves and the sport of Thoroughbred racing. Voted for by jockeys, the Woolf Award is one of racing's most prestigious accolades.

The youngest jockey ever to win 3,000 races and the youngest to win 4,000, Kent is a two-time winner of the Breeders' Cup, the winner of the Kentucky Derby in 1998 and 2000 and the winner of the Preakness in 1998. Among his winners is Gourmet Girl for owner Joe Massengale in 1997. He was inducted into the National Museum of Racing and Hall of Fame in 2004. He lives in California with his family.

FRED D. GRAY grew up in Montgomery, Alabama. While eligible by merit to attend law school in his home state, he was required to get his legal education in Ohio because in Alabama at the time, blacks were not permitted to enroll in law school. He returned to Montgomery in 1954 with a personal mission: "to destroy everything segregated that I could find."

As a sole practitioner less than a year out of law school, Fred Gray helped make history when he represented Mrs. Rosa Parks, who refused to give up her seat to a white man on a city bus, and thereby initiated the Montgomery Bus Boycott. The resulting case, *Browder v. Gayle,* integrated the buses in the city of Montgomery in 1956, and was ultimately the legal basis for the U.S. Supreme Court to strike down segregation on buses. Gray made a career of changing the social fabric of America regarding desegregation, integration, constitutional law, racial discrimination in voting, housing, education, jury service, farm subsidies, medicine and ethics and fulfilling the promise of the national judicial system. He was the first civil rights lawyer for Dr. Martin Luther King, Jr., and he represented Freedom Riders, the Selma-to-Montgomery marchers, the victims of the Tuskegee Syphilis Study, and many more.

In 1997, Fred Gray successfully encouraged President Clinton to make an official apology to the participants of the Tuskegee Syphilis Study, who were tracked by the U.S. Public Health Service for the effects of the disease but not informed they had it, nor treated properly. He has been the moving force in the establishment of the Tuskegee Human and Civil Rights Multicultural Center, which serves as a memorial to the participants of the Study, and which educates the public on the contributions made in the field of human and civil rights by Native Americans, African-Americans and Americans of European descent. He is the recipient of the American Bar Association's 2004 Thurgood Marshall Award.

TOM CASH earned his master's from California State University, Los Angeles. A longtime entrepreneur, his primary interest is children with special needs. He has taught special education students in the Los Angeles area since 1967.

B. MICHAEL YOUNG is president of the National Urban League of Young Professionals, and is one of the founders and founding members of NULYP. He is an executive for Verticalnet, a leading provider of management solutions to leading corporations. He is also a founder and managing principal for Copperfield Community Ventures, a firm that established strategic partnerships between the private sector and non-profit organizations. He received his bachelor's of business administration from Howard University and his MBA from George Washington University.

Michael has been an active leader and supporter of various other Washington, D.C., organizations, most recently serving as a founding board member of the Young Benefactors of the Boys and Girls Clubs of Greater Washington. His numerous recognitions include selection by America Online BlackVoices as one of the top ten young civil rights leaders in the country; by *Ebony* magazine as one of the "Top 30 Young Leaders of the Future" under the age of thirty; and by the "International Who's Who of Professional Management."

ACKNOWLEDGMENTS

The authors gratefully acknowledge the following friends and family who made this book possible:

The Massengale brothers, their wives and families; George Foreman; Guion S. Bluford, Jr., Ph.D.; Anjelica Huston; Kent Desormeaux; Rafer Johnson; Fred D. Gray, Esq.; Mr. and Mrs. Tom Cash; B. Michael Young; Adam Chromy, Artists & Artisans, Inc.; Julia Pastore, Harmony Books; Fred D. Massengale; Herbert Massengale; Oliver Massengale; Ollie Massengale; Lindell Massengale; Carwell Massengale; Dr. Lindell Massengale, Jr.; Johanna Massengale; Dorothy J. Massengale; Linda Smith; George McDonald; the Walton family; Roosevelt Walton; Clemmie Walton; Brandy Alaman; Lawrence Whaley; Floyd Dixon; Bennie Jewel Benette; Dr. and Mrs. Donald Anderson; D. A. Booker; Frankie M. Williams; Mr. and Mrs. Melvin Rogers; Jewel and Darvin Williams; Colleen Shaw; Janice Harris; Helen Shipp; Q. T. Minneweather; José deLima; Dr. William Digman; Brother Calvin Bowers, Figueroa Church of Christ, Los Angeles; Crystal Guy; James Greend; James Fisher; Barbara J. Crawford; Justine Caldwell Brown; Ollie D. Coleman Brown; Willie J. Brown; Curtis Brown; Josie Campbell; Mrs. Margie Perkins; Zaddie Adams; Dorothy Warren; Helen Clark Garcia; Ruth Clark Saunders; Annieruth Wilson; June Carnell; Tressa Tucker; Mr. and Mrs. John Wilburn; Foster Phillips; Charles B. Runnels, Chancellor, Pepperdine University; Monroe Watkins, Ph.D., and Carolyn Watkins, Ph.D., and FBN Affiliates; R. Wayne Hicks and Vercilla A. Brown, Black Data Processing Associates; Jaclyn Bashoff, Gray Angel Productions; Robert Pearlman, collectSpace; Debbie Baker, The Space Agency; Debbie Rowe, Special Olympics Southern California; Craig Dollase; Bob Baker, *Los Angeles Times;* Oliver Massengale Heshimu; Charles Massengale Sigidi; Rudi Groothedde, Managing Editor, *California Throughbred;* Scot Brown, Ph.D.; Edward Hotaling; Edward R. Ritvo, M.D., Professor Emeritus, The David Geffen School of Medicine at UCLA; Harry Hacek; Dierk, Renee and Meredith Toporzysek; Robin Miller; Akhilesh Daniel; Chuck Laustrup; Toni Freeland; Theatre Perception Consortium and the cast and crew of *North on South Central Avenue;* Laurie Stephens, Ph.D., The Help Group, Los Angeles; Hillary S. Meeks and *The Marshall News-Messenger,* Marshall, Texas; Bruce and Elizabeth Clow and family; Roger and Marcia Clow and family; Steve and Helen Dillon and family; Randy and Judy Miotke and family; Robin R. Ryan.